THE
MANAGER'S GUIDE
TO
INTERPERSONAL
RELATIONS

THE
MANAGER'S GUIDE
TO
INTERPERSONAL
RELATIONS

Donald Sanzotta

amacom

**A DIVISION OF
AMERICAN MANAGEMENT ASSOCIATIONS**

to
Laurie

Library of Congress Cataloging in Publication Data

Sanzotta, Donald.
   The manager's guide to interpersonal relations.

   Includes index.
   1. Interpersonal relations. 2. Organizational
behavior. I. Title.
HD58.7.S26   658.31'5   79-701
ISBN 0-8144-5508-5

First Printing

Preface

It has always been my feeling that good interpersonal relations depend largely on attitude—about oneself, about other people, and about the world and the conditions of human life. This collective attitude pervades all relationships, including the work environment.

As I have read the many books on interpersonal relations, they often missed or glossed over the attitude issue. They emphasized technique and the communication process without the basic understanding of people necessary to translate technique into human interaction.

It is for these reasons that this book is both general and specific in many ways. You will find chapters that focus on personality, and others that consider specific influence techniques. My objective is to offer both a fundamental understanding of people and their needs and an integration of concrete organizational situations and problems. In some ways you may find the topics rather diverse. This is intentional: Diversity is a central aspect of good interpersonal relations.

In this book I introduce what I believe to be a new concept in interpersonal relations—*therapeutic management*. I devote an entire chapter to the idea, and I use it as the centerpiece of my approach.

There are many actual cases throughout the book, most of which have dialogue designed to illustrate various principles of interpersonal relations. I have alternated this practical learning method with theoretical material to provide both theory and application.

At times I found very little source information on some of the topics. This served as a source of both motivation and frustration. Despite the difficulty of synthesis, the lack of data led me to believe that there exists a real need for this book.

I would like to thank all my friends and relatives who have encouraged my work through their valued support and reception of my first book, which served as motivation to write a second. I would also like to thank my able and understanding translator and typist, Barbara Cornell.

DONALD SANZOTTA

Contents

The time has come when if you give me any normal human being and a couple of weeks ... I can change his behavior from what it is now to whatever you want it to be, if it's physically possible. I can't make him fly by flapping his wings, but I can turn him from a Christian into a Communist and vice versa.

JAMES MCCONNELL, psychologist*

1

Introduction: Impersonal, Personal, & Interpersonal Relations

Many of us have a secret fear that what McConnell is saying is only the beginning of a new period of "enlightenment" in interpersonal relations. Not since the eighteenth century period of enlightenment, when new philosophical positions on individualism, universal human progress, and the scientific method developed, has such a significant leap in knowledge and values occurred. No doubt there have been major industrial and technological advances since then, but they have been quite different. This new change involves fundamental alterations in the ways people interact with one another—that is, interpersonally.

Those of us who are practitioners in the behavioral sciences know that if McConnell's statement is an exaggeration, it's not a very big exaggeration. Many of my colleagues are convinced that we are on the threshold of new breakthroughs in our knowledge of human behavior—and new problems. Genetic engineering, electrical stimulation of the brain,

---

* Quoted in James Flanders, *Practical Psychology* (New York: Harper & Row, 1976), p. 121.

1

psychoactive drug research, and mind control are a few of these new areas of discovery.

It is my belief that there is one other area of importance where new developments will have an equal or greater impact—interpersonal relations. Nowhere are interpersonal relations more complex and continuous than in the laboratory of human interaction known as the work environment. It is true that family and love relationships are more intimate and even more intense, but they usually involve fewer people and less time than relationships in the workplace, and no single individual has more interpersonal influence over the activities and day-to-day lives of people than the manager. Even powerful political figures don't have this kind of individualized personal power (except over their immediate employees). It is to this group—the managers of our working lives—that attention, information, and guidance must be given about the new field of interpersonal relations.

At present, managers are not equipped to understand and fully use either their own talents or the abilities of their employees. The formal education system does not prepare people to be managers. Courses in accounting, business law, and even organizational behavior do not address the problems of managerial skills and personality. On-the-job training does not deal with the development of these skills. Such on-the-job training teaches you which person in which department has which specific duties, and it usually takes from two days to a month to learn—then you're on your own.

This lack of training and understanding about people and work is really not new. As Frederick Herzberg has said, "Everyone asks whatever happened to the work ethic. The problem is we never had a work ethic." * Yes, we had a Protestant ethic, but what was it? It told us that hard work was good and that laziness was bad. It never once tried to look at the meaning of work or at the relationship between work and the health and well-being of the person. It never looked at work as enjoyable, and above all it never looked at the responsibility

---

* *The Managerial Choice to Be Efficient and to Be Human* (Homewood, Ill.: Dow Jones-Irwin, 1976), p. 33.

of an employer to make work part of the human growth experience for the employee. There was no ethic in work, socially or culturally, and to a large extent that is still the situation today.

Why this gap between work structure and worker? I think it is due to a combination of ignorance about what the manager's job really is and fear of power. Specifically, we have never adequately answered the question, "What is the job of a manager?" Instead, we have come up with definitions that center on getting others to perform. Such explanations can have useful purposes, but definitions of the managerial personality have always been very general and sociological in nature.

On a personal level, defining the job of a manager begins with a question that a colleague of mine learned as a judoist: "Do you know who you are?" Part of the answer lies in self-awareness, which we will discuss later, but part of it relates to *managerial roles:* As a manager, what are you supposed to do? What are you supposed to be? This is where the knowledge gap lies.

The fear that has resulted from this gap between the organization and the worker has developed from abuses of power and punishment. This is why McConnell's statement is so frightening. There is a fine line between general leadership and mind control—the differences between them are often matters of degree, not of type. Management has recently been trying to avoid this issue entirely. Competing centers of power ("counterpower"), such as unions, consumer groups, and government regulatory agencies, have contributed to the trend to ignore the power of the manager. Such controls on absolute power are, of course, valuable, but it is time we faced the fact that managing requires power. As one management scientist has pointed out, "Leadership inevitably requires using power to influence the thoughts and actions of other people." * We shall consider power in more detail later, but for now let us not fear the reality of it: It is there, it is necessary, and we must teach managers how to use it properly.

* Abraham Zaleznik, "Managers and Leaders: Are They Different?" *Harvard Business Review*, May–June 1977, p. 67.

Let us say that you, as a manager, have a role and that you have power within it—but how do you learn to use it effectively in dealing with people? There are all kinds of techniques for teaching human relations, and most of them aren't worth much. Even the best of training seminars have either short-term effects, or they initiate changes that are so minimal as to be insignificant. The boss goes away for a week to learn the latest techniques on how to handle people, and comes back a new leader, enthusiastic, understanding, and innovative—for a month.

We are going to be so presumptuous as to propose a new approach. *If you want managers to learn good interpersonal relations, teach them to be therapists!* Before you reject the idea, let us consider it further.

Which groups of professionals have the most knowledge and experience in working with personal and interpersonal problems? Which groups have spent the most time influencing behavior, attitudes, beliefs, and values, in a subtle and effective manner? There are several possibilities: (1) managers, (2) actors and advertising executives, (3) social psychologists, and (4) psychotherapists. In our approach, we will try to apply the findings of the last three areas to the actual practice of management, placing particular emphasis on the potential contribution of psychotherapists. Not that we want to make managers therapists as such—they often do not have the background or desire for such a role—but rather *we will adapt the techniques and skills of the therapist to the managerial role.* We do not want or need amateur psychiatrists in our organizations; therefore, the adaptation must fit the limitations and requirements of management, and not the other way around. This is an absolutely crucial distinction if we are to properly accomplish the mixture of the two areas of knowledge. The danger of abuse is significant, but the benefit of good integration is equally great. In training managers, we must use the best and most advanced techniques available, and when it comes to interpersonal relations, therapists know a great deal about behavior.

In the interest of balance, we shall also discuss the limits of therapy and how it is often made into more of a science than it really is. In fact, the only way to justify adapting such techniques to the exigencies of management is to maintain that *therapy is simply a special form of interpersonal influence.* A therapist tries to get a client to change an attitude or behavior through either direct or indirect techniques, which range from confrontation, threat/fear, and persuasion to support, suggestion, example, questioning, and passivity. Of course, managers may already use many of these techniques naturally, but that is no substitute for an organized, deliberate effort to adapt them for managerial training.

By the way, in making the assumption that adapted therapeutic techniques would be helpful to the manager, we are not saying that therapists would make good managers. In fact, I believe that they would make ineffectual and even incompetent managers in their pure roles. Nor are we even saying that they are the best practitioners of their own theories. Just as some of the best coaches don't make good players, some of the best theoreticians on interpersonal relations have great difficulty solving their own problems. Again, this does not mean that we cannot use their ideas.

The long-range benefits of an orientation toward interpersonal relations as therapeutic is consistent with the newer concepts of industrial mental health such as Herzberg's idea, "To be efficient and to be human." Humanization without efficiency is a nice idea, but it won't sell, and we are not proposing it. Rather, we are saying that humanization and productivity can be combined to form, perhaps for the first time, a work ethic; and the first step in this process is manager education and guidance. It is not an exaggeration to say that this could lead to a whole new approach to management.

There is a management theory, which has been around for some time, known as management by exception. Its basic premise is that routine responsibilities are *not* handled by managers, but that only unusual or exceptional matters come to their attention. With their broader background and wider perspective, managers can deal with these special problems, thereby allowing employees a certain amount of autonomy in their own jobs. This is a fine idea, but there are even higher levels of management strategies to which sophisticated interpersonal relations can contribute. After management by exception, the next level one might consider is *management by prevention.*

Management by prevention—foreseeing and avoiding problems—does not mean that you can control all the variables that affect your job. That would be unrealistic. But the more knowledge you have in advance about your role and your job, the better able you will be to successfully anticipate and head off problems. However, such a goal requires a level of managerial sophistication, at least in the area of interpersonal relations, that is far beyond current common practice. In fact, I would say that managers with sophisticated interpersonal skills are quite uncommon, and most managers cannot prevent problems that they have no idea might develop. In short, *management by prevention requires foreknowledge,* and although complete foreknowledge is not always possible, the ability to anticipate problems can be easily learned by training and education in human behavior and thereby in knowing what to expect from different people.

The sophistication required of predictive ability is central to the technological aspects of business. Nearly all the top corporations around the world have significant research and development facilities. Although good R&D cannot control all the technical, environmental, and consumer variables that a company may face, it still has a valuable predictive and preventive function in foreseeing and controlling problems. Why not an analogy for interpersonal aspects of organization and management? Instead of R&D in a technological sense only, why not apply R&D to worker–management development? I know there are isolated cases where extensive training and development have attempted to achieve goals in this direction, but most training is conservative, low-risk, skill training.

If training for interpersonal skills is ever to approach an R&D function, it must become more education than training by broadening the base of what corporate training is all about. Again, this has been done at times with upper-level executives, but it has received very little attention at middle and lower levels of management. I am not proposing that corporations take over the educational responsibilities of our society, but they could take the lead in two important ways: First, they could develop guidelines to be used by educational institutions for program development that would be more attuned to the nature of corporate jobs. Second, they could develop their own built-in systems for making interpersonal relations an R&D function.

Most high school and college graduates are totally unprepared to deal successfully with the political and informal organization structure in today's corporation. *They do not know how to get things done in an organization.* Not only have they never been taught this; but no one has ever told them that it was important information. They don't know what it means to relate to people and to get a job done at the same time. We have never taught them a work ethic, and we have never given them the interpersonal skills they will need on the job. Although many of them do eventually learn about organizations, this often is in spite of our educational system, not because of it.

Consider the classroom setting and ask how well it resembles our organizations. How much cooperation and teamwork are required in a classroom? What are the required behavioral traits? Competition, conformity, independence, obedience to authority, and social skills—yes, they are there, but now rank them in order of importance and ask which ones are stressed most. Does our list compare well with a similar ranking you would make for a healthy corporate structure? Mine doesn't.

It is not the responsibility of the corporation to correct this situation single-handedly, but corporate inputs into the educational system are needed and should be welcomed. Although corporate America should not set educational policy, one goal of education is to develop relatively happy and productive members of society, and often the critical ingredient is what an individual does for a living. Good interpersonal relations must be developed early in the education process, and explaining how these interactions are defined by the world of work is important in such education.

Perhaps we are being premature in expecting any kind of corporate leadership in vocational development before the corporations get their own affairs in order; internal corporate changes must come first. Not only must corporations know their own human resource needs, but they must also have jobs that require a total person. There is absolutely no point in educating students in good interpersonal relations and in how to get things done only to have them enter a work environment that allows or requires nothing of what they have learned. One may argue that if we were to compare the two systems, educational and corporate, the latter needs the most attention. It is the farthest behind, not in absolute terms, but because it has not yet fulfilled its own needs.

To lead the way, we must educate managers. We must teach them to be therapists and developers of people. This will raise the level of management practice. It will require us to develop a work ethic, provide guidance and models for our educational system, and make people more satisfied with their working lives. But it will work only if management believes in it. There are no shortcuts in this approach. It is not a formula; it is a process. With proper implementation, it could have a ripple effect throughout our whole society.

As you can see, my concept of interpersonal relations encompasses much more than the traditional ideas of human relations in industry. It is true that the essence of interpersonal relations is one person interacting with another person; but, when magnified and multiplied, these interactions apply to groups, communities, and societies. Hence, we will concentrate on one-to-one encounters, although the larger significance should not be discounted.

On the basis of our new definition of therapy from a managerial perspective, we must now explore what the development of the individual is all about. As a manager, before you can translate an idea like personal growth and development into sound interpersonal relations that result in cooperation and performance, you must first ask yourself about a number of preconceived ideas or attitudes that you may have about people. We will divide them into five categories: (1) self-development and other-development, (2) the person and the worker, (3) the Perimeter Model, (4) self-awareness, and (5) impersonal relations. In the remainder of the chapter, we shall consider each of these in turn.

SELF-DEVELOPMENT AND OTHER-DEVELOPMENT

Whom do you care about most? Your spouse, your family, yourself, your peers, or mankind in general? Some psychologists would claim that, despite what you say, your number one priority is *you*. Self-interest is the most funda-mental concern of a person, and to be able to reach out to others you must first have a healthy sense of self. Accordingly, if you take care of number one, the rest will follow.

This wouldn't be a bad theory if people grew up and lived in a vacuum. The fact is that *in order to develop a healthy sense of self, and in turn to reach out to others, you first have to be reached out to by someone else.* Among individuals it is a circular process: Without this prerequisite, the whole social structure breaks down, leaving isolated, hedonistic individu-als without any measure of collaboration.

The cause-and-effect cycle of self- and other-development is complicated by the problem that one does not automatically lead to the other. Some people never achieve enough self-development to reach out; others achieve self-development and leave it at that; still others reach out simply to fulfill their own self-interest, and wind up achieving neither. Very few people develop themselves enough to fulfill their own self-interest and still have the motivation and energy to help fulfill the self-interest of others. This is what we mean by other-development, and it is as uncommon in management as it is anywhere else in our society.

The absence of an other-development mentality among many managers is puzzling, given all the agreed-upon defini-tions of what managers should do. If they fail to develop the performance capabilities of the people who work for them, just what is it that they are supposed to do? In my view this is what being a manager is all about: If I can get you to develop yourself in such a way that it benefits you, me, and the organization, I have done my job and done it well. But that isn't easy and most managers aren't big enough to do it.

What we are talking about here is risk, commitment, and a genuine interest in other people. There is some question about whether such an attitude can be taught to someone. I think that, given certain limits which we shall discuss shortly, it is possible to identify and develop this attitude in people. Abraham Zaleznik calls people with this attitude *mentors* and defines them this way: "Mentors take risks with people. They bet initially on talent they perceive in young people. Mentors also risk emotional involvement in working closely with the juniors. The risks do not always pay off, but the willingness to take them appears crucial in developing leaders." *

The ability of a manager to be a mentor and thereby promote other-development often depends on circumstances and on chance happenings that make a person receptive to a mentor, but it also depends on the manager's ability to recognize such people and to communicate with them. This is what interpersonal relations is about.

THE PERSON AND THE WORKER

"When I go home at night, I leave my work behind." This is the most common self-deception among workers today. Anyone who believes that he is two different people is in trouble. The more complex your responsibilities at work, the more likely you are to carry them with you everywhere, but even basic assembly-line responsibilities have a carry-over effect.

Once and for all, let us abandon the mistaken belief that *what you do* and *what you are* exist as separate entities. *Over time, people tend to become what they do.* In any given circumstance, if you are asked to judge a person on the basis of what he says or what he actually does, which standard would

---

* Zaleznik, "Managers and Leaders," p. 76.

you use? Although you wouldn't ignore their words, it is their actions that most clearly reveal people's positions. It is true that we have simplified matters to make a point because we haven't considered the significance of internal conflict between one's own words and acts, but our point still stands: you ultimately act in certain ways by your own choice.

If you have remained on a job for 20 years, your entire personality has been influenced by it. Even if, for all 20 years, you gave as little of yourself as possible to that job, you were still shaped by what you did—namely, giving very little. As a result, in the end, you probably have very little to offer other people socially, at work, or at home. Your job has made you apathetic, shallow, or pessimistic about life, and you didn't start out that way 20 years ago. In more complex jobs, the positive or negative influence is even stronger.

Another related example is the attitude "20 and out"—"I will endure it for 20 years, then retire and do something I enjoy." This applies, provided that you don't die first and that you are willing to "sacrifice" 20 years of your life. Admittedly, fewer and fewer employees are willing to do this, but when it occurs it is based on the fallacy that the worker and the person are different. They are not.

If more people and more organizations realized the impact that careers and jobs have on the personality, much more concern would focus on the need for good interpersonal relations of the therapeutic type which we discussed before.

Perhaps the reader might react to the statement that the worker and the person are the same by thinking, "But I'm really so many different people in different situations." This is probably true, but the distinction psychologists make still allows for different people to be the same person. The distinction centers on the difference between a role and a personality.

"Personality" comprises the long-term pattern of behavior of an individual. One dictionary defines personality as "the totality of distinctive traits of an individual." A personality psychologist defines it more elaborately: "Personality represents the enduring properties of individuals that tend to separate them from other individuals. . . . What is important here is that personality expresses consistency and regularity." *

Within this pattern, people develop roles. Again, the dictionary defines a role in two ways, both of which serve our purpose: "1. A character or part played by an actor. 2. A function or position."

The worker and the person are *one* personality, and their actions involve two different roles. To preserve the integrity of personality, the aspect of "consistency and regularity" is carried from situation to situation. The healthy person maintains a sense of self throughout many roles, and although the roles change to fit the requirements of the job or situation, the personality changes only over time. The extent to which the personality can change will be discussed shortly, but in any case the change is very different from changes in role.

When people take on roles, they have the choice of being themselves and fulfilling the requirements of "a function or position," or they may act out a role that is not representative of their underlying feelings, as when an actor plays a part. People who behave this way are often called phonies because they conceal their real personalities and try to project to the world an artificial image of themselves.

If good interpersonal relations are to be achieved, it is absolutely essential to understand personality and some of the roles people play, and it is our goal to develop an understandable set of principles and guidelines on both topics throughout this book.

THE PERIMETER MODEL

A great deal has been written about the powerlessness and ineffectuality of middle managers in today's large organizations. From an interpersonal standpoint, I don't believe a word of it. There may be lack of control over budgets, wages, overall working conditions, technological advances and limits, and marketing success, but for the middle manager power-

---

* Lawrence Pervin, *Personality: Theory, Assessment, and Research* (New York: John Wiley & Sons, 1970), p. 3.

lessness in relating to others is, and always has been, primarily an individual problem. By this statement, I don't mean to discount sociological and environmental influences over personal behavior, but such factors involve wide perimeters within which a variety of actions may develop.

It may be true that early childhood experience (for example, separation from a parent as a result of divorce) may make an individual insecure about relating to people, but such a circumstance does not justify the kind of attitude expressed in such a statement as "I don't believe a manager should be too friendly with employees." In one sense, the history of such a person is a general condition, and the attitude is a specifically selected point of view on which there may be several hundred variations within the same historical or developmental background.

Of course, such an assumption about human behavior is a compromise between the two philosophical extremes of determinism and free will. We are saying it is not a choice of either one or the other; rather, it is a mixture of both. Without expanding this into a rambling debate on the causes of behavior, it seems imperative to establish the basic attitude that a manager must develop if successful interpersonal relationships are ever to be achieved.

Underestimating the effect of your own underlying attitudes about what makes people tick will often lead you either to be unaware of people who don't behave according to your expectations, or to be surprised and disappointed by them. For example, suppose you have an employee who performs well, but is somewhat abrasive, rubs people the wrong way, and is making your department look bad politically in the organization. In dealing with such a problem you have basically three possible choices:

1. Ignore it. It doesn't mean your own leadership is in question just because one of your people has a personality problem.
2. Sidetrack the person into a set of responsibilities that are less sensitive and visible.
3. Try to change the person.

Whatever choice you make, your basic assumptions about the determinism–free will continuum will show up, however subtly; furthermore, it would be fairly easy to place you on this continuum on the basis of which choice you made. We might plot the choices in a linear fashion:

Determinism   **Free Will**

We are really asking one fundamental question: Do people have the ability and capacity to change their own behavior, or are there powerful predetermined factors that make such efforts superficial?

Back to our example of the abrasive employee. If, after considering all the circumstances, you were to select option number two, then you would clearly have a deterministic attitude. If you were to select number three, your belief in the individual's capacity for change would be clear. The first option is somewhere in between: You believe in the independence of your own free will, but you are deterministic about other people. Keep in mind that any one situation does not necessarily profile your overall attitude on where *all* people fit on this continuum, nor does it indicate how your assumptions might vary from situation to situation, but it does make you aware of the possibility that this most basic and insidious form of predisposition is important in how you relate to people.

Rather than use the continuum for the determinism–free will question, I would prefer the perimeter model that I mentioned earlier. It would look like the model shown in Figure 1. The limits of personal change would be circumscribed by the development within the social environment. Your childhood and past adult experiences and development, as well as your cultural and organizational environment and the conditions that either promoted or limited your personal growth, lie in that outer circle. Within the inner circle are the choices that a person can make in a more or less open manner.

Figure I. The perimeter model.

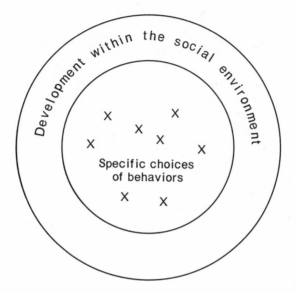

That is, the interior represents an individual's capacity to make relatively easy changes in personal actions and attitudes. *It is primarily this inner circle that concerns us in our discussion of interpersonal relations.*

This perimeter model will be the basic format, and it will set the tone for most of the ideas and techniques that follow. We shall also address many of the structural and organizational influences on human behavior in order to reach a better understanding of interactions between people.

SELF-AWARENESS

It has been my experience that many people want to understand their spouses, bosses, employees, and their friends and adversaries, but they often miss a·crucial step in their efforts—they forget to understand themselves first. This is probably the oldest piece of psychological information around, and most of us agree with it but don't really understand why the "know thyself" directive makes sound psychological sense.

There are basically three reasons why self-awareness is intricately related to good interpersonal relations. Dudley Bennett suggests two of them: "People are not usually aware of how their behavior looks to others. Sometimes they wonder why they behave the way they do, but more often they wonder why *others* act as they do." *

Knowing how you are perceived by others is the initial step in evaluating your impact on people, and feedback from other people is one of the most objective forms of information about you, since there are really only two places feedback can come from—yourself and others.

Second, attempting to understand the strengths and weaknesses of others before you have confronted and accepted your own strengths and weaknesses will undermine your objectivity. Psychoanalysts call this projection. As a defensive mechanism, you unconsciously attribute to others traits or characteristics of your own that are unacceptable to you. For example, if you are unconsciously upset with yourself about your disorganized work habits, you may make a projective statement like, "I never seem to be able to get the people who work for me to plan ahead and to get themselves organized." It's fairly easy to recognize projection when it occurs in other people, but to see it in ourselves requires a great self-awareness.

Third, whenever we talk about the virtues of self-awareness, we are making a value judgment. We are saying that it is better to be aware than unaware. I am convinced that this is true, but I also believe that there are many, many people who don't want to be self-aware. To them, the process is too painful, not worthwhile, or even destructive. When we advocate self-awareness, we are making a judgment that such awareness offers more alternatives for growth than does a lack of awareness.

Given the above rationales for self-awareness, one of our

* *TA and the Manager* (New York: AMACOM, 1976), p. 1.

major goals in developing concepts of interpersonal relations is to emphasize the fundamental principle that *good interpersonal relations begin with good intrapersonal relations.*

IMPERSONAL RELATIONS

There is one more assumption that must be examined before we continue: What about inappropriate dependencies? How personal should your relationships be in an organization? Again we may look at the extreme positions. Many of our organizational interactions involve either no real emotional commitment or dependencies that inhibit personal growth. The extremes are intense passive relationships at one end, and shallow manipulation at the other.

Contrary to what you might expect, our position is not a compromise between these two extremes; rather, it is a third alternative. Involvement or lack of it is not really the point. The real questions center on issues such as these: What *kind* of involvement? What are its goals? What are the costs and benefits? Once the appropriateness of the involvement has been determined, the question of too much or too little is not relevant because if involvement is appropriate, then there is no such thing as too much. It's true that appropriateness may mean a certain level of involvement, but that is quite different from the question, "Should I or shouldn't I get involved?"

We can take such a position because of what our concept of helping others really means. If I help you only to the point that you become dependent on me, I am in effect an emotional junkie—I have taken advantage of a need within you, and I haven't gone far enough to allow you to satisfy that need on your own. Lawrence Brammer puts it this way: "The aim of all help is *self-help* and eventual self-sufficiency. What I have emphasized is that much of our growth is the result of self-help and self-searching, rather than something done to or with us." *

The real issue, then, is how to help others help themselves,

* *The Helping Relationship* (Englewood Cliffs, N.J.: Prentice-Hall, 1973), p. 5.

using "healthy dependencies." Some psychologists and psychotherapists would say there is no such thing as a healthy dependency, that it is a contradiction in terms. Others believe that certain emotional dependencies are a sign of stability, openness, and identity achievement. This is my own position, and we will take up the merits of the case later, but for now let us say that one of my major assumptions is that in interpersonal relations, getting emotionally involved with others makes them stronger, not weaker.

A final note on involvement: You will be able to get emotionally involved with others and still perform effectively only to the extent to which you are secure about yourself. Part of this relates to self-awareness, but it also goes beyond it into self-acceptance. *It is one thing to know yourself, it is another to like what you know,* and the two do not automatically occur at the same time. Almost every therapist and psychologist would agree that you will not be able to fully reach out and accept others until you have "reached in" and accepted yourself.

Now that we have clarified some of our basic assumptions about people and their needs, we can begin to study the problem in depth.

Let me introduce myself. I am a man who at the precocious age of thirty-five experienced an astonishing revelation: it is better to be a success than a failure. Having been penetrated by this great truth, my mind was now open for the first time to a series of corollary perceptions. . . . Money I now saw was important; it is better to be rich than to be poor. Power I now saw was desirable; it was better to give orders than to take them. Fame I saw was unqualifiedly delicious; it was better to be recognized than to be anonymous.

NORMAN PODHORETZ

2

The Politics of Power

Interpersonal influence has been important throughout human history. For example, commerce increased rapidly as cities began to grow, because for the first time large numbers of people could deal with one another face to face. Today, this concentration of direct contacts in cities is typified by the options of managers in midtown Manhattan who, within ten minutes' walking distance, have direct access to over 150,000 people. It will be a long time before telephone, television, or computer communication can replace the efficacy of direct one-to-one contact and the individualized power that it offers.

This power, of course, can be used or abused, and we must consider both possibilities objectively. Our goal may be to facilitate smooth interpersonal transactions that allow for the success of varied objectives in an organization but, realistically, interpersonal influence, as part of any transaction, can also involve a disruptive power struggle.

The only people who underestimate the value of power are those who don't have it—their criticism is merely a rationalization to justify their own feelings of powerlessness. ("If I cannot have it," they might say, "then I don't want it anyway because it is corrupting.") Of course, it is possible for people with or without power to overestimate its value. For those who don't have it and who overestimate its value, acquisition of power becomes a consuming drive, whereas those who have power and who put too much emphasis on it often become tyrants.

In organizations, underestimating the value of interpersonal power means several things: First, that you probably don't have any, and want to pretend that it is unimportant; second, that you aren't going to be as successful in performing your job as you might be; and third, that your career isn't going anywhere. Furthermore, until people recognize that interpersonal competence and the power that accompanies it are key elements in job success, they will be unlikely to pay much attention to the development of such skills.

In any managerial role, sensitivity (caring and understanding how others feel about themselves, their work, or their families) is good management, but it is not in itself power. Sensitivity can give you power but it alone does not ensure good leadership or the respect of others. However, knowing how to use power is in itself leadership. This may sound cold and manipulative, but management is manipulation of capital and of labor. And, in its positive applications, that kind of manipulation is the essence of leadership.

In his book *Management and Machiavelli,* Antony Jay points out the interpersonal aspect of leadership:

> Machiavelli called his book *The Prince,* and not something like *The Art of Government,* because he saw success and failure for states as stemming directly from the qualities of the leader. Success and failure for corporations also stem directly from the qualities of their leaders.*

No matter what the size of the organization, power ultimately rests upon the individual and upon the one-to-one encounter.
Before we can discuss communication and therapeutic

* Hinsdale, Ill.: Dryden Press, 1967, p. 26.

management, the premise of power must be accepted. Without it, we may have group therapy and harmony among individuals (although we might also have anarchy), but we will not have an organization that gets things done.

There is a risk, of course: The techniques we are to discuss, if finely developed, can give a manager tremendous power to mobilize resources and achieve work goals. The risks of exploitation are present, and there is no use denying them. Perhaps the most effective way of protecting people from interpersonal exploitation is to make them as healthy, strong, and independent as we can—that is, to develop counterpower. Counterpower is the ability to face others from a position of strength and confidence. Such an approach may raise the power struggle to a new level, but historically this has benefited the weak more than the strong. For an example, labor unions have undoubtedly escalated the power struggle between workers and management, but their counterpower has resulted in much less exploitation of the worker today than there was 100 years ago.

Milton Erickson, a world-renowned hypnotist, is an individual who has an extraordinary amount of interpersonal power at his command. *It is possible for Erickson to shake hands with someone and to so transfix their attention that he can put them into a preinduction or preliminary state of hypnosis. That* is interpersonal power. As a manager, you have probably shaken thousands of hands with all types of professionals and associates. It is a ritual, often of seemingly little importance, but in viewing it so nonchalantly, you have missed a very significant form of interpersonal influence.

You are probably not a hypnotist, so how can you expect to have this kind of power? Perhaps you cannot, although Erickson himself believes that given the proper training and conditions, almost anyone can exert this kind of influence. Nevertheless, an awareness of interpersonal influences and their dynamics can markedly increase your power, even if you never become an Erickson.

The quotation at the beginning of this chapter illustrates that it is better to be a winner than a loser. Without simplifying this into Vince Lombardi-isms, it is clear that Americans view winning as the ultimate goal. Sometimes we have even gone so far as to define losing as winning, in order to have a no-lose contest: The old canard, "It's not whether you win or lose, but how you play the game, that counts," has been used for generations to assuage the disappointment of losing teams and to convince them that in losing they have actually "won."

Even organizational conflict resolution has spawned theories that call everyone a winner. There are lose–lose strategies, win–lose strategies, and win–win strategies, all of which can be appropriate at certain times, although a win–win strategy is always best. This is an agreeable approach to conflict resolution, but it is also unrealistic. Within organizations, there are too many clear-cut win–lose situations for us to pretend that winning is not important.

We are not suggesting a survival-of-the-fittest approach to management, although this does exist in many organizations. We are attempting to be realistic about opportunities and limitations that you as a manager and that organizations as a whole must face. Promotion and career development is an example. Antony Jay discusses how the "best and the brightest" theory of power and leadership can be a fallacy:

> The cream always rises to the top. This happy domestic metaphor can be a great comfort to good corporation men, and the nearer the top the more comforting they will find it. But not all corporations are milk bottles. . . . It is, in fact, by no means inevitable that the best men will go to the top of the firm. And even if you pursue the milk metaphor, you will find that cream has another property as well as rising to the top: It also goes sour quickest.*

The "best and the brightest" approach typifies the American ideal: hard work and talent equals success and winning. This is true—sometimes. In other cases, the most technically competent engineer will be passed over and someone else will be given that special project, or the manager who has

* *Management and Machiavelli*, p. 168.

solved production problems in the subassembly area will not receive proper recognition. Most important of all, the top executives whose decisions affect the entire organization may have a value system that is not in the best interests of the company or of society. So, how do these people get to the top? What are the crucial ingredients in achieving power and success? In my opinion, interpersonal relations is the key.

In *Psychology Today*, Rosabeth Kanter discusses what makes people effective managers, supervisors, and team leaders.* One of the most important factors is credibility. *Credibility means competence plus power.* This translates into the ability to get results. People who had this credibility were listened to; their phone calls were returned quickly; and, in general, others believed that they could back up their words with actions. In particular, "upward credibility" was important—that is, to have credibility with their own employees, managers first had to have it with their bosses.

Having credibility with your boss identifies you as a winner. It labels you as confident and capable, and conveys a sense that you will be promoted, which enables you to attract and keep good staff people. Qualified employees do not like the idea of working for a manager who is going nowhere, and if they suspect this about their boss, they will either lose their motivation or move elsewhere.

We must, therefore, address an important question: How do you achieve credibility? How do you become part of the "fast track"? The three most common methods of climbing the organizational ladder are building a personal "empire" within the organization, attaining high visibility, and finding a powerful "godfather" to sponsor one's own rise to power.

First, powerful leaders need to build their own suborganizations, or empires, either in the form of special physical facilities—offices, production areas, and branches—or by means of organization charts and reorganizations. By reorganizing, a manager puts into key positions people who will enhance his *own* performance and image. It represents a real change and is, in many cases, an improvement. Reorganizing

* "Power Games in the Corporation," *Psychology Today*, July 1977.

also allows a leader to allocate rewards such as new titles and new job responsibilities. This in turn increases the leader's personal credibility and power.

Again, as Machiavelli pointed out, if a prince is to govern a diverse empire, he must place key and trusted people in distant lands; otherwise, he will waste all his efforts trying to keep the conquered peoples in line. The analogy to corporate life is not remote. If a manager is to compete with peers—and win—control is essential to performance, and having one's own suborganization stabilizes an emerging empire.

A second component of credibility and power is visibility. People who are on the way up have an instinct for the visible. They are able to seize upon opportunities to enhance their images and profiles in an organization. They will take some risks but, ideally, not risks that could lead to failure. As one manager put it, "The thing to do is to make it *look* like a risk but to actually have it in your back pocket. You need the attention that comes from taking a risk, but the security of knowing you can't fail."

In short, visibility means being noticed by people who count—namely, higher-level executives. However, your efforts at gaining visibility must not be all appearance and no substance. A sense of immediacy must accompany visibility, and your actions must be relevant to current or pressing organizational problems. Without relevance, you may encounter one of two problems—doing something important that is not recognized as such, or getting the reputation of a publicity hound who does things only for the sake of visibility. Also, the instinct for visibility must be accompanied by a good sense of timing.

The third and most important point is the effect of both your empire and your relevant visibility on one particular person who is in a position of power higher than your own. *The godfather system is alive and well in American organizations today.* It exists in government, in education, and in all areas of private enterprise.

Political party bosses are godfathers, college professors who get students into graduate schools are godfathers, and

executives who get managers promoted are godfathers. Godfather is simply a less sophisticated and more political version
of the term *mentor* used in Chapter 1. They mean the same
thing.

Having friends in high places can offer several advantages.
First, they can stand up for you in meetings at which you are
not present to defend yourself. Second, they can give you in-
side information, thereby allowing you to circumvent the established procedures of the bureaucracy. Often, if you have to
go through the "chain of command," your initiative can be
slowed down or derailed but, with a godfather, you have access to a whole different level of power. Third, as a result of
what is often called "reflected power," they can give you a
strong, positive image. This is a signal to others that you have a
sponsor, which gives you credibility and the power to get
things done.

A godfather can be an important factor in your career by
increasing your interpersonal power. But how does one find
such a person? And how does one eventually become a godfather oneself?

To find a godfather, or mentor, or sponsor, your visibility
must be directed at someone who has a personality similar to
your own. For someone to make you a protégé, that person
must strongly identify with certain things about you and must
have an attitude typified by such statements as, "this is the son
I never had," or "this is the person who can, with my help, be
everything I never was." Your efforts must be directed only at
those powerful people who see you as very much like themselves! Don't miss the point about relevant actions, or else
many of your attempts at visibility will simply cause you to be
viewed as a boot-licking, favor-currying, weak manager. You
must be very selective about whom you choose as a potential
godfather, and even then there is a risk. But your desire to be
sponsored will not in itself cause someone to decide to become your mentor; you must also be visible, develop an organization of your own, and tackle a relevant problem that
offers some, but not too much, risk to you.

Another indirect way to be recognized by powerful people

in an organization is to be a godfather yourself to lower-level employees. You can increase your visibility simply by having your subordinates be your best salespeople. This will give you an even more valuable reputation than that of simply having leadership quality, because it will demonstrate in a forceful and tangible way that you have the ability to transcend your own self-interest and to be concerned about both your fellow employees and the organization. *"Winning" managers are those who see other people's growth as being in their own best interest.*

There are many objections to the practice of promoting a subjective, favorite-son system in our organization. For example, what about women? If godfathers see themselves in younger managers, and if most of the mentors are men, how can they look at women and see themselves? The answer is that they can't. For many women, this has closed the door to higher managerial levels for years, but there is some evidence that it is changing. It seems that when women acquire sponsors, it occurs for different reasons than when men do so. Some executives sponsor women to show that they are enlightened and that they have a new consciousness about the female manager. Others act as sponsors to show that they are able to handle an unusual management situation and, at the same time, to solve a corporate quota problem. Thus, they are, in effect, creating their own visibility for *their* godfathers.

And what about the basic unfairness of the godfather system? Are we simply to be pragmatic and amoral about this? Is it true that if the name of the game is power, then you have to grab for it as best you can? Not necessarily. There are rules, and they are not just the rules of the jungle.

To deny the existence of interpersonal influence and power serves no purpose; we must face it honestly. The hypocrisy of our present system is in itself justification for change. On the face of it, we maintain formal rules, strictly delineated promotion policies, and official channels of communication; yet, the informal and interpersonal route is widely used. A close comparison between a bureaucratic system and a godfather system shows one major similarity: Both systems regard results as the ultimate test of effectiveness, and both are based on performance. Superficially, one may appear to be more subjective than the other, but any claim that our present system promotes equal opportunities is nonsense.

There is no such thing as equal opportunities in interpersonal relations: Every opportunity is a multivariate of specific circumstances and individual conditions. There is such a thing as structural discrimination, but it deals with stereotyping and arbitrary labeling on a system-wide scale. But here, I'm referring to discrimination based on personal likes and dislikes, a kind of discrimination more fundamental than that based on race, creed, sex, or national origin. It means that of two managers who work for me, I might like one better than the other and believe one to be more effective and competent than the other, and that I will be a mentor to one and not to the other. How can you change this kind of discrimination? I would maintain that you cannot, and perhaps should not.

This is not to say that a manager should not use objective criteria to judge performance and promotion issues—there is a danger that subjective feelings will override objective facts. But, in the long run, such decisions don't pay off, and that is the safety valve of the entire system: If, because of personal friendship, I sponsor an incompetent, I will damage my own credibility. The only way this self-corrective mechanism might not work is if *everyone* in management were incompetent and were promoting only people who were images of themselves. I find that assumption unrealistic.

Do not disregard objectivity, but don't assume it to be the only factor in management. By definition, interpersonal relations have subjective, emotional qualities—this is what gives interpersonal communication its richness and substance. In an effort to make individuals more objective decision makers, we have spent many hours training and developing managerial skills. That in itself is fine, but the problem is that it has come at the expense of another type of skill training: *We have not taught managers how to use subjective information.* As a result, many of them are incompetent in handling interpersonal relations, and thus have neither credibility nor power.

In addition to helping managers accept subjectivity, I want to persuade the reader that there is a connection between interpersonal relations, a therapeutic attitude, and power. I hope to make that connection clearer when I examine each of these topics.

Images from the mass media, sexual identities, and parental styles all contribute to the development of a rigid and narrowly defined view of power. These influences can promote insensitivity to the more subtle and gentle types of power influence, which are no less effective than a hardheaded approach. Let us illustrate this with a specific example: the relationship between managers and masculinity.

In the opening paragraph of his book, *The Male Machine*, Marc Fasteau describes an idealized image of a good manager:

> The male machine is a special kind of being, different from women, children, and men who don't measure up. He is functional, designed mainly for work. He is programmed to tackle jobs, override obstacles, attack problems, overcome difficulties and always seize the offensive. He will take on any task that can be presented to him in a competitive framework, and his most important positive reinforcement is victory. . . . His relationship with other male machines is one of respect but not intimacy; it is difficult for him to connect his internal circuits to those of others.*

This male machine is everywhere, but nowhere is he more pervasive than in our organizations. He is subtle, he is not very different from all the other machines, and he aspires to power in a set, mechanical way. Although he is easy to figure out, he is not easy to change, nor is it easy to work around him, since he is everywhere and is continually reinforced by his peers.

It can be said that this is the type of person who gets things done in business today, that he can be a machine at work and a person at home. However, this is the worker-individual dichotomy described in Chapter 1, and it just isn't valid. The

---

* New York: Dell, 1975, p. 1.

male machine does get things done in our organization, but compared to whom? If an organization is dominated by male-machine godfathers who develop and promote people similar to themselves, how can other approaches to interpersonal behavior get a chance to be tried out? Is power an "either-or" proposition—that you either have male-machine power and are respected, or you are dominated by others and are therefore considered organizationally ineffective?

I would like to propose a new type of "mentor power" for managers: It is for Winners, it requires leadership, and it takes time, effort, and talent to learn it. We will call it *therapeutic power*. It demands the ability of a mentor because it requires a concern for less qualified talent. It is therapeutic because it involves the use of subtle techniques and requires an attitude of managerial leadership that is both benevolent and effective. It is an approach that is both work- and person-oriented.

Therapeutic power is not a technique for dominance, nor is it basically passive. *The use of therapeutic power causes others to feel stronger, not weaker.* It causes them to feel *independent*, not *dependent* and submissive.

David McClelland of Harvard University conducted one of the most enlightening experiments on how the use of power promotes feelings of powerfulness in others. Some time after John F. Kennedy's assassination, McClelland exposed groups of business-school students to a film of the President's Inaugural Address. This film must have been a very moving experience for such an audience at that time. Meanwhile, another group was shown a film explaining aspects of modern architecture. He expected to find that the students who saw the Kennedy film would feel submissive, obedient, and loyal. Instead, he found that they felt powerful, strengthened, and uplifted by the experience.

What is suggested here is that a leader does not *compel* followers to submit by sheer force of personality, or what is sometimes called the personality power syndrome; rather, leaders arouse *confidence* in their followers. They inspire people by developing and expressing goals which, at least to some degree, the people themselves aspire to. In effect, leaders say to people, "You are strong and capable, and you can accomplish these goals."

But the question that arises is, "How does a manager help employees to feel more powerful?" For too many managers this question is a threat to their authority, leadership, and power. But paradoxically, the more you protect your supposed power, the less you will actually possess in the long run.

It would be a misinterpretation to assume that we are suggesting that managers turn the organization over to the employees, nor are we suggesting that employees be led to think they have power that they really do not possess. Rather, we are saying that there is no interpersonal power possible without the consent and confidence of those affected by it.

Helping employees to feel more powerful means being a mentor to them. It means recognizing their strengths and teaching them to recognize and develop these positive abilities. It means that rather than ignoring their weakness, you teach them both to recognize such weaknesses and to work at correcting them.

Although there may be some employees who are unreachable, managers often write off employees because of their *own* insecurities about being successful mentors. Again, we are back to the problem of risk: The more risk you believe to be involved, the less likely you will be to offer genuine power options that will develop employee talent and, in turn, make you a mentor.

Therapeutic
Management

In an idealized conception of a good manager we see a profile of a person who is a good leader, a good teacher, a good follower, and a good person. To this list I will add yet another desirable trait: a good manager is also a good therapist. The meaning of this statement depends upon our ideas of what therapy is all about. We can define therapy in a broad or narrow context. We can view it as a subject that encompasses defined clinical doctrine, or as a discipline based on little solid information. We can see it as the vehicle for either fundamental or superficial changes in behavior.

WHAT IS THERAPY?

The dictionary defines therapy as any treatment designed to bring about social adjustment. This could mean almost any life experience that has a positive effect on social adjustment, such as achievements, avoidance of failure, exercise of skills and abilities, social recognition, acceptance, or enhanced control. Each of these events could facilitate social adjustment and thus be called therapeutic. Furthermore, none of them need take place in the traditional context of a doctor-patient setting.

Therapy can also be viewed as any self-correcting process that is, in itself, an adjustment. Many psychologists would agree that coping behavior, even when it doesn't work or is neurotic, is at least an attempt at therapy. Again, in a broader context, Ralph Heine makes this point: "All human behavior is in one way or another concerned with manipulating the self or the environment to provide psychotherapy when it is needed, and practically speaking, this is rather frequently." *

Therapy can be defined as any process, event, or outside agent that promotes or enhances personal growth. Again, this can mean life experiences, both good and bad; significant others, such as relatives, friends, employers, or professional counselors; or self-evaluative processes such as reflection, introspection, and behavior analysis. The essential elements of a job most certainly offer these opportunities, but whether they are growth enhancing and therapeutic depends on a number of factors:

> The working environment
> The job itself
> Your status, recognition, and level
> Top management
> Your boss
> Your peers
> Your employees
> Yourself

In addition to the various aspects of a job that can be therapeutic, this wider definition of therapy should take into account those experiences that are not therapeutic, such as withdrawal, reduced self-esteem, impulsive and compulsive behaviors, and self-defeating attitudes.

A further refinement of our assumptions about therapy is provided by Ralph Heine:

> Psychotherapy can be seen either as a transparently simple phenomenon that everyone intuitively understands and has practiced, or as a confused, incredibly complex process well

* *Psychotherapy* (Englewood Cliffs, N.J.: Prentice-Hall, 1971), p. 2.

beyond the reach of current scientific understanding. Considered merely as a collective term for events that have a demonstrably salutory effect on one's state of mind, psychotherapy is readily comprehensible to everyone. In this sense of the term, the catalog of potentially psychotherapeutic human experiences is endless.*

Of course, we do not need such broad definitions for our purposes. After all, we are primarily concerned with managers and their performance, but such definitions increase the chances of convincing many managers that the concept of therapeutic management does have a place in the organization.

THE CONCEPT

Since the idea of therapeutic management has not yet been developed in a body of literature, it is our task to translate conventional psychotherapy into a theoretical approach that can be used by management. Such a theory must take into account the general background of managers—that they are not trained psychologists—and must take great care to define the limits of acceptable intervention. Thus, it must include the idea of job-relatedness, and it must attempt to synthesize widely divergent points of view within the fields of professional counseling and psychotherapeutic training. Finally, in order to give the idea of therapeutic management practical significance, the translation process must take into account the interpersonal relations aspect of the manager's job.

It is with these considerations in mind that I shall explain my approach to this concept. First, my presentation must be eclectic, drawing from various sources, yet at the same time emphasizing those psychotherapeutic techniques that have particular value when translated into management language. In the chapters on technique, there will be a review of theories drawn from Sigmund Freud, B. F. Skinner, Albert Ellis, Eric Berne, Abraham Maslow and, in particular, Carl

* Ibid., p. 1.

Rogers. When it is appropriate, I will identify individual sources, but it is not my primary objective to present a fully cataloged description of each theorist, since most managers don't have the time or the motivation to be scholars on personality. Here, I would like to emphasize that you will be presented with one person's individual view of these various techniques—I make no claims to have the definitive interpretation of these ideas.

Also, I will not present "pop psychology" approaches as if they were accepted practices. All the theories I discuss have been in use for some time, and have been accepted by large groups of serious professionals. Hence, there will be no discussion of Primal Screaming, Marathon Encounters, Rolfing, est, or nudity. Not that any of these methods are wholly without merit—some of them do have some redeeming qualities—but in order to discover those positive qualities, you would need a detailed individual account of each therapy, and that is not my objective here.

WHAT THERAPEUTIC MANAGEMENT IS NOT

Therapeutic management is *not* straightening out the lives of those less fortunate than yourself. *It is not giving advice.* It is *not* attempting to change someone's personality, and it certainly is *not* treating mental illness. Yet it is a type of counseling that is badly needed by most managers, who are constantly asked to straighten out people's lives, give advice, and even modify personality traits. Managers may feel uncomfortable about it, and rightly so, but the kind of counseling they do in appropriate circumstances may be no less uncomfortable for others. What passes for counseling in many managers' definitions might not be recognized as such by a professional counselor.

Counseling or managerial therapy is limited by two important factors: (1) organizational interest and job-relatedness, and (2) the abilities of the manager. These two points are the basis of my concept of therapeutic management.

Job-relatedness is not easy to define (in Chapter 1, we discussed the danger of separating the person from the job); since all sorts of outside influences affect job performance directly. There is, however, a solution to this problem. *Therapeutic management always considers self-development its main objective.* Therefore, therapy in the most active sense is played down. Tinkering is expressly not the purpose of therapy, managerial or otherwise. As Peter Drucker points out,

> An employer has no business with a man's personality. Employment is a specific contract calling for specific performance, and for nothing else. . . . We have altogether not the slightest idea how to change the personality of adults . . . management development and manager development are not means to "make a man over" by changing his personality.*

Therapeutic management is not merely a set of mechanical techniques. One eminent therapist, Otto Rank, was fond of saying that his technique of therapy consisted of having no technique. This allowed him the flexibility to consider the almost limitless variety of human personality. In this regard, a therapeutic attitude must also be developed: There is no single correct approach, nor is there any quick remedy for solving problems in interpersonal relations. This does not mean that there are no guidelines, but rather that the guidelines must be flexible for both the manager and the employee. This is pointed out well by Altman and Taylor:

> The ability to communicate with one other person requires a highly idiosyncratic, well-tuned, and synchronized communication system. It is difficult to believe that such communication can happen all at once. If this is correct, then what appears to pass for intimacy, genuineness, and respect for the integrity of others may be nothing more than a new level of superficial exchange which is only a substitute for the very things that had been rejected.†

---

* *Management, Tasks, and Responsibilities* (New York: Harper & Row, 1974), p. 424.
† Ivan Altman and Donald Taylor, *Social Penetration: The Development of Interpersonal Relationships* (New York: Holt, Rinehart, & Winston, 1973), p. 187.

This quotation, as you may have guessed, also touches on the issue of manipulation. Communication must above all else be sincere; otherwise, we just have new techniques for the same old exploitation.

Also, therapeutic management does not deal with mental illness. Some of the adapted theories are derived primarily from therapists who treat personality disorders, neuroses, and psychoses. Some may argue that given the proximity of this illness approach, it is best not to give managers tools and skills that will be used to give the impression that they are capable of treating people with psychiatric problems. I have two responses to this argument: First, it is important for managers to be able to recognize when they are dealing with a psychiatric problem. (See Chapter 4, "The Person," for a full statement of this problem.) Second, a manager can expect to encounter serious psychiatric problems on the job infrequently, although the incidence of interpersonal problems will be quite high. I have concluded from this risk-benefit analysis that offering adapted therapeutic tools to the manager makes sense.

To further minimize the risk, I am presenting those therapeutic tools that offer the smallest possibility for iatrogenic, or physician-caused, harm. For example, I shall discuss the unconscious only from the point of view of understanding defenses, not for purposes of interpreting or removing defense mechanisms by means of psychoanalytic techniques. As Joel Kovel states: "Therapy gets more ambitious as it attempts to go beyond the limits of counseling into the incursions made by the unconscious, and it also gets more problematic, more liable to bog down, or even to harm." *

THERAPY: SCIENCE AND ART

Although I wish to avoid both pop psychology and treatment of mental illness by the manager, I also want to avoid the shortcomings that preprogrammed answers might provide. Even within therapy itself, and among its practitioners, there

---

*A *Complete Guide to Therapy* (New York: Pantheon Books, 1976), p. 48.

are serious reservations about this. For example, Abraham Maslow states:

> I share with many other scholars and scientists a great uneasiness over some trends (or rather misuses) in Esalen-type education. For instance, in some of its less respectworthy adherents, I see trends toward anti-intellectualism, anti-science, anti-rationality, anti-discipline, anti-hard work, etc. I worry when competence and training are by some considered to be irrelevant or unnecessary. I worry when I see impulsivity confused with spontaneity. I worry when people, especially young people, overlook the fact that the proponents of spontaneity, for example people like Aldous Huxley or Carl Rogers, are themselves highly disciplined, hard working people who think of true spontaneity as the consequence of much hard work, as the reward for high personal development.*

Furthermore, it is not as though we are asking managers to practice a science for which they are untrained. Maslow acknowledged this in particular when it came to applying the sensitivity training method too broadly. "I consider much of the Esalen-type education to be the application of a science which does not yet exist," he said.

Of course, to say that psychology does not have a scientific attitude or methodology is too general a statement, and brings us closer to that "anti-science, anti-discipline" approach Maslow warns against. On the other hand, it is important to guard against jumping to unwarranted "scientific" conclusions.

The dangers of distorting this concept of therapeutic management are significant enough to justify careful and detailed qualification of the idea. It would be too easy to propose a revolutionary approach to job enrichment, participation, and interpersonal harmony in the work setting. There is a great temptation to become the kind of "phony Messiah" described by Kurt Vonnegut:

* "Humanistic Education vs. Professional Education: Further Comments," *New Directions in Teaching*, Spring 1970, pp. 3–10.

"Oh, this business we've got now—it's been going on for a long time now, not just since the last war. Maybe the actual jobs weren't being taken from the people, but the sense of participation, the sense of importance was. . . . Even then there was a lot of talk about know-how winning the war of production, not people, not the mediocre people running most of the machines. . . . They were participating in the economy all right, but not in a way that was satisfying to the ego. . . . Things, gentlemen, are ripe for a phony Messiah. . . .

"Messiah?"

"Sooner or later someone's going to catch the imagination of these people with some new magic. At the bottom of it will be a promise of regaining the feeling of participation, the feeling of being needed on earth—hell, dignity!" *

I don't wish to be a "phony Messiah" by advocating the idea of therapeutic management—it is only a component of organizational leadership. I believe it to be an important component, but it is, after all, an idea based on aspects of a manager's job, and its principles are based on a developing science whose conclusions have not been fully tested. Psychiatry itself is often questioned by people in the profession. Therefore, any theory based on its principles must be regarded cautiously. This point is made by Frederick Herzberg:

I have always believed that psychiatry is an amateur profession. . . . Most of their knowledge consists of clever insights into the frailties of human nature, blown up in psychiatric terminology to be no more than any observant person already knows. . . . I do not deny or deride psychiatric insights. But I do feel that psychiatry is open to rip-off, or over-the-counter remedies disguised as medicine.†

My intention is to present both the art and the science of therapeutic technique in a way that managers can use and understand, without going beyond their abilities or the requirements of their jobs.

* *Player Piano* (New York: Avon Books, 1967), pp. 92–94.
† *The Managerial Choice*, p. 33.

WHAT THERAPEUTIC MANAGEMENT IS

First, therapeutic management is a collaborative problem-solving effort. It is designed to develop the manager or employee by creating the environment where the personal growth required to do a job well can be nurtured. From a management development point of view, Peter Drucker explains:

> There is, typically, the first-class engineer who judges himself to be a good manager because he is "analytical" and "objective." Yet, to be a manager requires equally empathy, ability to understand how others do their work, and a keen sense of such "nonrational" factors as personality.*

This deficiency is present in every organization, and in its confusion and anxiety over the problem, management has fallen for all kinds of human relations gimmicks because it has not been fully aware of its own objectives. The objective is simple, as Peter Drucker states: "The development of a manager focuses on the person. Its aim is to enable a man to develop his abilities and strengths to the fullest extent, and to find individual achievement. The aim is excellent." †

Development for these purposes can only be defined as therapeutic. To create an environment that fosters "empathy," "individual achievement," "a sense of personality," and "excellence" is growth-oriented and promotes social adjustment.

If therapeutic management is of benefit, then how do you become a member of such a team? In general, we are talking about a mentor mentality, interest in the development and growth of others, and respect for the "person." The fundamental goals of such an approach are to:

1. Reduce anxiety in the work environment.
2. Open channels of communication.
3. Enhance the self-esteem of the people in that environment.

* *Management, Tasks, and Responsibilities*, p. 425.
† Ibid., p. 426.

This kind of approach does *not* require a person of superhuman abilities, although that may appear to be the case from the following passage, which at first glance seems to list the qualities of the ideal therapeutic manager:

> I am a most skillful individual. I am considered superb at conversation. My broad knowledge enables me to discuss almost any topic you choose, and be stimulating. I can be serious, hilarious, informative or light. I am responsive to you and considerate of your feelings. If you feel even the slightest offense or discomfort, I will switch to another topic without arousing your anger. In fact, perhaps my greatest virtue is that you are completely safe when you relate to me. I will not embarrass you. I will not punish you. I will not humiliate you. I am your tireless friend. I have only one possible fault: I am possibly too skilled in my relations with people. With my tireless energy, I am ready to take over your social functions . . . I may have done so already.*

Who is this wonderful person? It is not a description of a person at all. It is a description of television! The point is that therapeutic interpersonal relations do not mean perfect relationships; in fact, the imperfections may make interpersonal relations even richer. Carl Rogers has said that it is encouraging to know that "imperfect human beings can be of therapeutic assistance to other imperfect human beings." Therapeutic management includes:

Humanization of the workplace
Participatory management
Job satisfaction
Flexitime
Cafeteria-style rewards
Cooperative bargaining
Human resource development

All the terms that imply autonomy and flexibility at work are therapeutic concepts. More generally, the phrase being used today is Quality of Working Life (QWL).

* Flanders, *Practical Psychology*, p. 233.

The definition of QWL is so general that it can mean different things to different people. Michael Maccoby, the director of the Harvard project on Technology, Work, and Character, asks what QWL really means: "Are people resources to be developed for some purpose other than their own well-being? If so, for what purpose are they being developed? The development of human beings, in terms of their capacity for reason, mutual aid, and creative activity, should be the purpose of our system, not the means to some other goal. *

In this regard, we cannot sell humanness as a disguise for productivity. If this happens, as it has in the past with some other human resource development projects, the effort will fail. Organized labor, for one, will not support it. Unions will not cooperate if they perceive it to be a new technique that management has devised as a means of "getting more for less." Opposition by labor was a major factor in defeating Edward Kennedy's 1972 Worker Alienation Act. (However, Rep. Stanley Lundine (D–N.Y.) recently proposed the Human Development Act, which attempts to improve both economic productivity and the psychological quality of working life. In Rep. Lundine's words, "We must learn to work 'smarter' rather than harder.")

Thus, QWL, or any of the concepts included in my idea of therapeutic management, will not sell itself—there are too many vested interests that oppose it. For this reason, we must also find a way to put these concepts into practice on an interpersonal level. The interpersonal level is more subtle and less threatening than organizational levels, but it can make as lasting and profound an impression as structural change. It means focusing on one-to-one encounters, altering attitudes on an individual level, and changing assumptions about work to a personal value system approach.

When the idea of therapeutic management is examined closely, it is not as exotic as it may first seem to be: It simply means developing a conceptual framework in which managerial attitudes and assumptions will be formed. If we concentrate on the basic assumptions managers bring to a job, we can

* American Psychological Association, *APA Monitor*, Washington, D.C., Nov. 1977.

shape ideas in a fundamental way. The connection between therapeutic management and the quality of working life can be seen in this excerpt from a speech given by Al Warren, who is the Director of Personnel Development for General Motors. He is discussing QWL, but note how closely his ideas resemble therapeutic management concepts:

> There are a number of ways of defining the term, but I think it fundamentally comes down to extending adulthood to the work place. By and large, industry in the past has treated employees as children, telling them what they can't do rather than helping them to achieve what they're capable of. Employees want to be treated as adults, with respect and dignity. They want meaningful jobs that give them the opportunity to use their abilities and grow. We're talking about creating an atmosphere that makes employees feel their ideas are needed.*

People want to be treated with respect and dignity on an interpersonal level, but by treating them as adults in one-to-one encounters and then giving them depersonalizing jobs, we make our organizations seem hypocritical. Just as you cannot say that you respect a person and then turn around and treat him disrespectfully, you cannot tell employees that they are a meaningful part of an organization and then place them in jobs that deny the very idea of making a significant contribution.

As evidence of this contradiction between therapeutic interpersonal relations and nontherapeutic jobs, here is what a telephone operator had to say:

> I like to know my work is done well. But my job isn't to talk to you like a human being anymore, I'm nothing but a machine now. I have exact phrases I'm allowed to say. I'm a machine but only until they can find a real one to take my place.†

---

* From a report by the National Center for Productivity and Quality of Working Life (Washington, D.C., Manuscript, 1977), p. 5.
† Ibid., p. 2.

This type of alienation on the job makes it necessary for therapeutic management to be organizational as well as interpersonal.

TRENDS

In their efforts to increase the scope of organizational involvement in helping employees get treatment for alcoholism, drug addiction, and irrational disturbances, companies are moving toward the therapeutic management concept.

For example, Kemper Insurance recently expanded its Personal Assistance Program, which for many years had dealt with problems of alcoholics and drug addicts, to include employees suffering from personal and emotional problems. Supervisors are now instructed to contact the Director of Health Services about employees who show signs of erratic behavior, extreme tension and stress, instability, outbursts of temper, chronic lateness, absenteeism, and so on. After an evaluation the director may refer the employee to an appropriate organization, such as a family counseling service, psychiatric clinic, or social service agency. Employees themselves are encouraged to call on the director; they are given assurances of strict confidentiality, and are guaranteed that no written records will be kept on what they say.

Another example is Kennecott Copper's program called IN-SIGHT, the alphabetical translation of its phone number, which operates 24 hours a day, seven days a week. Troubled employees, or their families, can dial INSIGHT to get immediate referral to the director of the program, who is a psychiatric social worker, for consultation and possible further outside help.

Programs like those at Kemper and Kennecott are emerging from increasing acceptance of the belief that alcoholism, drug addiction, and emotional disturbances are illnesses that can be treated, and that the company has a responsibility to help employees get such treatment. The success of such programs, I believe, depends on the manager's ability to recognize a troubled employee, and we have devoted several chapters of this book to that goal.

The next step in this trend toward therapeutic management is twofold: (1) developing the idea of what constitutes therapy into a broader concept of interpersonal relations, and (2) training managers in techniques of interpersonal relations that are of therapeutic value. Here we must emphasize that we do not want those who follow this approach to be subject to charges of practicing psychotherapy without a license or without proper training. The therapy idea translated into management means providing an atmosphere of growth and development and being ready to help others and to engage in crisis intervention, if necessary. We can follow the example of an even more restricted and potentially volatile area—the practice of medicine by nonprofessionals.

Programs that train *anyone* in cardiopulmonary resuscitation are becoming increasingly popular. Other programs offer to teach anyone how to take a person's blood pressure. Despite the potential dangers of crisis medical care, many doctors are in favor of a more informed and competent public. At Columbia Medical Care Plan in Columbia, Maryland, mothers have learned to take throat cultures from their children. In diagnosing the cultures, the mothers agreed with professionals in 136 of 137 paired home and clinical cases.

In fact, this idea goes further than just simple intervention. Dr. John Renner, Chairman of the Department of Family Practice at the University of Wisconsin Medical School, says:

> I've put together some little surgical kits. If self care is promoted by a trusted provider who respects his patients, many things are possible: removing foreign objects from the eye, suturing cuts, even, in an emergency, performing a tracheotomy.*

If medicine can move in this direction, then therapeutic techniques can readily be applied in the workplace, since their potential dangers are much less serious. In this context,

* Robert Yeager, "Doctoring Isn't Just for Doctors," *Medical World News*, October 1977, p. 48.

therapeutic management is not a radical idea; in fact, its widespread use may be overdue.

In either medicine or psychotherapy, no one has yet agreed on the lines of demarcation between professional and paraprofessional practice. Some experts say that half-knowledge is dangerous in that it promotes a false sense of security among its practitioners, which will lead to unreported serious problems being exacerbated by delays or maltreatment.

However, there is also a more optimistic viewpoint about therapeutic interventions. Some experts say that increased medical and psychological knowledge will allow people to report symptoms more meaningfully. They maintain that an informed public will recognize serious problems more readily than an uninformed public, and that this will speed intervention and save lives. This is, of course, my position. I hope to support it in the chapters that follow, but, more important, I hope that the real support comes when these techniques and guidelines are translated into successful practice.

In the past, a scientific understanding of human behavior was unknown, but recently, psychology and the behavioral sciences have prospered and have attained a more widespread acceptance and recognition. The course for the future must be to integrate into daily life the knowledge of human behavior that we have available today. In this way, personal growth and development—in the family, at school, or on the job—will be a common feature of the human condition.

*The lobster grows by developing and shedding a series of hard, protective shells. Each time it expands from within, the confining shell must be sloughed off. It is left exposed and vulnerable until, in time, a new covering grows to replace the old.**

GAIL SHEEHY

4

The Person

Most managers don't have a very clear idea of what defines a personality. Ideas about how people behave are plentiful in any organization, but they are often a combination of personal experiences and perceptual inaccuracies. Just as there are a multitude of "personality psychologists" in our organizations, there are also training techniques designed to help the manager be a better judge of people, such as interviewing approaches and performance appraisal forms. Most of these objective methods have failed, and managers still evaluate personalities by intuitive and subjective criteria. Given this entrenched behavior, it is our position that training and educational efforts might be better directed not at increasing a manager's objectivity but at working from the other direction to make the subjective process of personality assessment more acute.

The very first principle that must be understood is so basic that it is often overlooked: *All behavior has a cause.* This premise, of course, assumes that there is a sense of order and sequence in behavior. What it does not assume is that persons are always aware of what causes their behavior, nor does it imply that behavior is always rational.

Psychologists have only scratched the surface in determin-

---

* *Passages* (New York: Dutton, 1976), p. 1.

ing what causes specific behavior in people. As to what causes entire *patterns* of behavior that make up a personality, the answers are primarily theoretical and unclear. For our purposes, I shall divide the personality into three fundamental kinds of expression: *cognitive, affective,* and *behavioral.*

Cognitive processes are thought processes. They are rational, reasonable, and they involve the intellect. Developing a budget, designing a piece of equipment, or setting objectives are cognitive activities. *Affective processes are emotional.* They are visceral responses or gut reactions, such as anger, anxiety, and depression, or joy, satisfaction, and enthusiasm. The feelings that result from getting a promotion, selling a big contract, or helping an employee to feel better are all affective responses. *Behavioral processes are actions.* They involve observable motions, gestures, or spoken words. Checking on production, visiting branch offices, or submitting reports are behaviors.

Together, cognitive, affective, and behavioral processes make up a person. Unfortunately, these functions do not occur separately or individually. Rather, there is an infinite number of possible interactions among all of these, although these interactions do follow some general guidelines. First, most people—and managers in particular—underestimate the effect that emotions or affective processes have on the cognitive and behavioral aspects of personality. For example, consider an emotion such as anxiety. In its milder form, it can stimulate your thought processes, but in its severe form it can give you a powerful mental block, which will prevent any productive thinking. Thus, anxiety can either improve your performance or make you lose coordination and paralyze you with fear.

More generally, emotions affect thought processes and behavior involved in making judgments and decisions. Emotional influences on judgment are often not recognized as such by the person experiencing the reaction, because cognitive processes tend to protect the individual from emotionally painful revelations. Personality psychologists call these protections *defense mechanisms.*

Defense mechanisms are important factors in understanding why people act the way they do. They are reactions designed to protect self-esteem or guard against undue anxiety. They generally operate in such a way that the people exhibiting them are not aware of their existence; as a result, a manager who can detect these processes in others may gain insights into the behavior of those people that even *they* do not have.

In an effort to protect themselves, people rationalize both their own behavior and the actions of others. A rationalization is an excuse fabricated unconsciously to justify a person's actions or situation. It shields that person from the painful realization that he may in some way be inadequate or wrong. You can hear rationalizations on the job all the time:

"I wouldn't take that job if they gave it to me."

"If I could only get good people . . ."

"I didn't want that project assignment anyway."

Often rationalization extends beyond the self to others. When this occurs it is referred to as projection—attributing to others ideas or behaviors of your own that you find unacceptable. For example, someone who feels guilty about his own prejudicial beliefs may tell a coworker, "You know, one of your problems is your inability to accept people as they are." People heard to remark that "nobody is really interested in doing a good job anymore. . . ." may feel anxious about their own work quality. The list of defense mechanisms is a long one. It includes:

Reaction formation: This involves beliefs or actions that are the opposite of the way a person unconsciously feels. Unacceptable feelings are denied by overreacting to them: "I am not prejudiced; if anything I bend over backward . . ."

Repression. This is unconsciously motivated forgetting. Through repression, unacceptable thoughts are blocked out: "I don't remember your ever saying anything about those quality standards."

Intellectualization. This means removing the emotional impact of an idea or behavior and substituting abstract verbiage. For example, in response to a negative performance review: "Management science has yet to develop an objective performance appraisal system." (Thus, "You'd better not evaluate me negatively!")

The overuse of defense mechanisms is the single most significant inhibitor of open and harmonious interpersonal relations. Then why do defense mechanisms exist in the first place? The most widely accepted theory is that defenses accomplish two purposes: (1) They distort reality slightly, making circumstances and perceptions easier to accept emotionally. (2) They preserve or enhance self-esteem.

In the first instance, these slight distortions of reality are highly individualized so that people "see what they want to see." Thus, two people who have two different sets of perceptions do not communicate from the same information base, and in operating from different assumptions, they arrive at separate, independent conclusions. In addition to this, there is the tendency not only to distort one's own information, but to then project *other* people's distortions. The result is often a breakdown in communication. Sometimes it's a wonder that we can relate to each other at all!

However, on the positive side, let us emphasize that although distortions of perception do create problems, such distortions are not total, so that it is still possible for us to remain objective in several ways. Feedback from others can be an important grounding device—if people tell you good and bad things about your behavior and attitudes, you can get usable information by which to judge your own perceptions. Of course, this kind of feedback will only be effective if you are receptive to it—it is for those "who have ears to hear."

Another way to test your idea of objectivity is to evaluate events. By reflecting and analyzing your successes and failures and the positive and negative outcomes of your actions, you can begin to determine how real your perception of reality is, and make the necessary adjustments in your behavior.

One final method of testing reality is simply by acting— doing things that make it clear to you what is real and what is merely your sensory perceptions. This is what Freud meant when he said that work gave us our idea of reality. However, this "testing of reality" does not refer to psychotic delusions, but rather to the everyday problems that arise as a result of one person's seeing things one way, and another person's seeing things differently. Both may be sincere and yet disagree, as the following example illustrates.

This case occurred in a factory setting in which an employee with five years' experience was working on a cutting machine for plastic piping. As the supervisor walked down the next aisle, he thought he saw the man working without the guard down. He also thought he saw the man tap the guard into place as soon as the man thought someone was watching. The supervisor approached him and said, "Jim, as I was walking by in the next aisle I saw you working with that guard up. Now, you know that could be a serious breach of safety regulations—you might even get a three-day layoff."

"What are you talking about? I don't have that guard up," Jim replied. "Where were you standing? I didn't see you near here. You know that there are two sets of machines between me and that other aisle. I mean, if I had it up, I would admit it. Sometimes I do get moving so fast that it does ride up, but not lately, because the machine hasn't been running right since the new blades were put in."

Who is telling the truth? Is the supervisor experiencing a distorted perception perhaps because when he worked on the line *he* lifted the guards? If that were true, it would be a form of projection. Or is the employee merely lying? Is it conscious denial, or is he rationalizing his lack of awareness without remembering what really happened? Certainly we don't know the answers to these questions unless we are objective observers. Neither of the participants are objective; hence, their defenses distorted reality for one reason or another, thereby creating a problem in interpersonal relations.

By what specific methods can a case like this one be resolved? First, the supervisor can try to determine if his perception was correct by watching Jim work the machine during a certain period of time, and seeing if the employee kept the guard down or not. This is what is meant by reliability of an observation: Do the observed actions remain the same over time? Secondly, the employee can pay more attention to how he acts on the world—namely, the machine—and how his movements actually do affect the guard. This may not completely solve the problem of who was right, but we cannot expect to get a precise answer to that question when we are in the process of trying to make two people's separate visions of reality compatible.

The second purpose of defenses is to preserve or enhance self-esteem. Understanding this aspect of defenses is even more important to the practical life of the manager than the reality problem. *If you want people to be open and less defensive with you, don't attack their self-esteem.* Although this guideline appears simple, people violate it all the time, sometimes without realizing it; then they're surprised when others become defensive for no apparent reason. Beware of making statements like the following:

"But that's not the point."

"I wish you wouldn't always say . . ."

"You don't really believe that?"

"I really don't understand how you could . . ."

When you say things like that, it is easy for the other person to accuse you of adopting a parental attitude. In certain contexts, even the most innocuous comment can be seen as a threat, depending on the *defensiveness threshold* of the person at whom the remark is directed.

A defensiveness threshold is determined by the inherent personality strengths or weaknesses of the individual, by the nature of the challenge, and by the circumstances surrounding the challenge. Some people seem almost naturally open and undefensive about almost anything, and others are uptight about almost everything. Given these variations in defensiveness threshold, it is easy to step over the line without really intending to do so and, as a result, to create a communications problem.

These thresholds may not always involve personality traits. It is possible to threaten a person's self-esteem indirectly by attacking his role behavior. The following conversation is an example:

Ron, production supervisor (to plant manager): "As I see it, my problem is an overzealous quality control department. Until the last few months we hardly ever stopped production. We're doing the same good work we've always done. But lately Sylvia's been stopping everything if one defective part comes down the line. Sure we have a reject pile, but it certainly isn't any bigger than it ever was."

Sylvia, quality control supervisor (to plant manager): "Are you going to stand for that? It's no wonder the reject pile reaches to the roof, in view of his low expectations. The rules clearly state that quality control can halt production if we get more than five rejects an hour. Just mentioning the problems in the weekly report didn't do any good."

Clearly we have here a power struggle—a conflict that is organizationally built into the roles of production and quality control supervisors—but fundamentally, at this point at least, self-esteem is on the line. This is particularly true for the production supervisor, Ron: By rejecting production parts, Sylvia is indirectly telling him that he is not a good supervisor. She is doing this objectively, but, from his perspective, it is a threat to his occupational identity. She, on the other hand, either doesn't see this or doesn't care, which will only make the situation worse.

What should be done here? The answer is surprisingly simple. The plant manager should say something like this:

"Now look, you both have jobs to do, and both of you are doing them well, or you wouldn't be in this situation right now, but in each of your efforts you have overlooked our common objective—to turn out a good product in enough quantity to make money for everyone concerned. How can we work together on this? Ron, what can you do to help quality control? Sylvia, what can you do to help production? . . .

Notice that the manager did not attack the two supervisors directly, but instead substituted a "productive" defense for their "nonproductive" defenses by removing the mutual threat to the self-esteem of the two individuals.

The idea of attempting to channel or to substitute defenses

is worth pursuing. People have defenses for a purpose—to protect themselves from undue anxiety. If these defenses do not work well, the person may suffer debilitating anxiety. *People need their defenses.* It is only by abandoning their defenses *themselves* that people become more open and objective. It is the role of the psychotherapist, not the managerial therapist, to help people shed defenses. Attempts to confront people and break down their defenses before they are ready to do so can make the situation worse by causing them to retreat even further. Therefore, you should *respect the person's self-esteem and the defenses that protect it and, whenever possible, attempt to reduce threats to that esteem.*

Efforts to protect our self-image and self-esteem often center on our concept of what is normal. As a manager, your beliefs about what constitutes normal behavior influence your judgments about your employees and the general interpersonal relationships you have with them. We all have a mold into which we would like people to fit and, when they don't, we react with disappointment or hostility. This rigidity about other people's behavior creates an environment that promotes defensiveness.

Based on these discussions of interpersonal behavior, we can construct a "normality" checklist:

It is NORMAL . . .

to want interpersonal power.

to want to be a mentor or a protégé.

to want to be accepted.

to want to be different or special.

to change your feelings and your attitudes.

to want to be consistent.

to feel inferior to some people.

to respect and resent authority.

It is NOT NORMAL . . .

to hate yourself and everyone else.

to be emotionally numb.

to stop growing and changing.

to expect everyone to be like you.

to be too much of a conformist.

to be too much of a social deviant.

to be self-defeating all the time.

to want to be passive and submissive all the time.

As can be seen, our idea of normality is broad-based and rather open, but it is more: It is weighted toward the idea that *healthy people like themselves and do things that enhance or enrich their lives.* If you as a manager do things that enhance a person's positive self-image, you will improve your interpersonal relations, but if you threaten or denigrate that person's self-image, your interpersonal relations will suffer.

Now, this seems simple and straightforward enough: Everyone is positive and healthy, and we all make a lot of money for the company. Unfortunately, this idyllic situation doesn't exist in the real world in which we all live and work.

Everyone has rackets. Rackets are negative behaviors and feelings that have benefits. There are all kinds such as: depression, sadness, inadequacy, anxiety, confusion, anger, helplessness, fear, and guilt. You may say that no one benefits from being depressed or feeling helpless. Well, then why do they? They can't help it? Are they forced into it? By whom? The only thing I can force you to feel is physical pain. I cannot force you to feel guilty if you choose not to.

You choose to engage in these rackets because of past experiences, and because you get what is called secondary gain. When you are depressed, your primary emotion is negative— you feel bad. Secondarily, however, you may get attention, special consideration, or reinforcement for your belief in how worthless you are. Being depressed relieves you of the pressures of working, playing, and loving.

Of course, these rackets are not really positive; you only think they are. We often hear about productivity on the job, and how people use only a portion of their potential abilities. If we could measure the amount of psychic energy that is wanted in racketeering, we would be amazed that there is anything left over for the positive things we do manage to accomplish.

The basic purpose of these rackets is to protect what we consider to be our very fragile self-image. We don't want to confront experiences that are too new or too demanding. Our self-image might get bruised or even seriously injured. This is what Dr. Abraham Maslow has called the Jonah syndrome. In the Old Testament story, Jonah was swallowed by the whale because he was afraid to preach The Word, as God had instructed him to do. He felt he was not worthy or able to do it: He feared his own potential for greatness; he feared being overwhelmed by the experience.

This shows that we often fear our best behavior as much as we fear our worst behavior. We often experience conflict and ambivalence when we see the highest possibilities in other people. People whom we view as being very competent and successful make us feel uneasy, confused, jealous, and inferior. They threaten our self-esteem, and we react defensively. Fearing the best in ourselves and in others can prevent us from enriching our lives. It prevents us from being effective mentors or protégés. In addition, we always have negative behavior as a final explanation for our failure to become as fully developed a person as we might.

Once you are aware of how racketeering operates within yourself, you can also spot it in others. Every one of your employees has some sort of racket going on the job, and as a result they are not doing their best work.

THE ADULT PERSONALITY

Psychologists have devoted a great deal of attention to personality development in infancy, childhood, and adolescence, and have paid some attention to old age. Not until recently, however, have they paid much attention to the 45 years in between. New research has focused on the psychological and social tasks and challenges that people face as they proceed through adulthood.

In the past we have looked at physical and personality changes of children in stages of one to three years. Yet we assumed that after adolescence, life was one long stage. Part of this oversight stems from the different rates of change. For example, if you observe a two-year-old on one occasion and then see the child again in six months, you will notice dramatic changes. However, if you meet a 25-year-old one day, and then see the same person six months later, you may not notice any difference. It is true that the stages of adulthood last longer and are therefore less obvious, but they are nevertheless just as real and as important as those of childhood.

As Gail Sheehy points out,

> Everything that happens to us—graduations, marriage, childbirth, divorce, getting or losing a job—affects us. These *marker events* are the concrete happenings of our lives. . . . The underlying impulse toward change will be there regardless of whether or not it is manifested in or accentuated by a marker event.*

These marker events are also referred to as stages. Although there has been a lack of attention to adult stages of development, some work had been done in the 1950s by a few theorists such as Erik Erikson. His theory of personality development postulates that the entire life span has eight stages, three of which occur in adulthood.

Erikson believes that *intimacy* is the central challenge of young adulthood. By intimacy, he means a close bond with another person, usually (but not necessarily) a spouse. The alternative, he believes, is *isolation,* or the lack of lasting emotional attachment to another person. In middle adulthood, the major task is *generativity,* the desire to have an impact on the next generation. This can mean guiding one's children or making a general contribution to society. The alternative is *stagnation* or lack of any real feeling of substance to one's life or one's lifework. In later adult years or old age, Erikson emphasizes the concept of *integrity,* the chance to look back at one's life with a feeling of accomplishment and satisfaction. The alternative is a continuation of stagnation leading to *despair,* or a feeling that life was not really worth the trouble.

Drawing on the work of Erikson and that of other researchers, and using her own interviews with adults at various stages in life, Sheehy has developed the following detailed picture of the stages of adult life.

Ages 18 to 22. In this period, the identity crisis of late

* *Passages*, p. 29.

adolescence continues. (The term "identity crisis" was coined
by Erikson.) People attempt to establish who they are and
what values and beliefs they hold independently of their parents and of other powerful adult role models. Concern about
intimacy may also develop.

Ages 22 to 28. People have substantially answered the
"Who am I?" question and now begin to get on with the business of life, such as getting started in a career (not just a job),
selecting a mate, and developing a lifestyle appropriate to
their needs and personal inclinations.

Ages 28 to 32. These are often years of uncertainty and
doubt about the choices made in the twenties. During this
period people may decide to make changes, such as getting
married, getting divorced, or changing careers.

Ages 32 to 35. After a period of change and transition at
about age 30, the early thirties are years of "settling in."
People become more pragmatic and rational about their lives:
They buy houses, advance in their jobs, and begin to be concerned about raising families.

Ages 35 to 45. The "settling-in" stage may continue
through the thirties, but at some point during the 35-to-45
decade people may experience a midlife crisis, which is often
precipitated by the sudden realization that one's life is half
over. This revelation, when combined with an examination of
what one has really accomplished thus far, may cause one to
ask what life really means. At this point in their lives, people
often have to face the fact that many of the goals and ideals
they once held may never be realized. Even if they have
reached the pinnacle of success, they may feel a letdown, and
may be skeptical about future accomplishments. This is a time
when people ask themselves the question, "Where do I go
from here?" Midlife, therefore, is a time for reassessment of
life goals and purposes. As Sheehy says, "If you recognize that
you will never be president of the big-city bank, you can get
on with becoming branch manager in your favorite community
and maybe find your greatest pleasure in becoming a Little
League coach or starting a choir." * Many theorists believe

* Ibid., p. 247.

that the midlife crisis is as important and as potentially disruptive as the adolescent identity crisis.

Ages 45 to 60. If people avoid or bypass the midlife crisis,
these years of their lives can be characterized by stagnation.
Many people who don't go through a midlife crisis lose their
drive to continue in later life. In the fifties, a midlife crisis can
be even more severe and painful than in the forties. However,
successful negotiation of the midlife transition can lead to a
feeling of renewal and satisfaction that can extend well into
old age.

It should be pointed out that much of this research is very
new, and therefore tentative. Not everyone goes through all
the stages: Some may proceed in a different order, others may
go through the stages at a different rate and time in their lives.
The idea here is to offer a general guide to these marker
events. As you attempt to understand people better, your
knowledge of adult stages of personality development and
change can be useful.

AGING AND PERSONALITY

We all tend to have our own ideas about what older people
are really like. We often think of them as rigid, cautious, irritable, wise, patient, forgetful, or senile. However, most of the
research on old people indicates that the personalities of older
people tend to be as diverse as the personalities of people at
any other stage in life. There are old recluses and old activists,
old people who are happy, and old people who are depressed.
One study found that people's personalities at age 70 were
much more affected by what their personalities were at age 30
than by the onset of aging.

Many have claimed to have discovered the secret of
longevity, but few of these assertions have been substantiated.
One 106-year-old man recommends weekly Bible study—and
drinking a fifth of whiskey twice a month. The people of Vil-
cabonba, Ecuador, where extended longevity is common, live
in a tranquil valley, have an ideal climate, and eat a low-
calorie diet with little meat. However, they are also in the

habit of drinking two to four cups of rum and smoking up to 60 cigarettes a day.

Conflict over the role of aging employees has been going on in our organizations for some time. For example, Fred has been with the company for 40 years, but he hasn't come up with a new idea in years, and he is making almost three times the salary of an entry-level employee. New employees may have great potential and fresh ideas, and be a financial bargain, but they may need time to understand organizational life, and to learn to do their jobs properly. Also, many of them are likely to change jobs within the first two years. Fred, on the other hand, does have a lot of experience. He has dealt with problems in the organization that none of the new people know about. But, of course, much of Fred's experience is obsolete; ways of doing things change, his education is no longer relevant, and he has not kept up with new developments in the field. This example illustrates a crucial point: Companies must continually provide incentives for all its employees, no matter what their age, to remain actively involved in their jobs.

STRESS AND PERSONALITY

Any of a number of suicide-prevention services in major cities around the world handle an average of 1,000 calls a day. In a quiet German rural area, a modern clinic operates to guide overstressed young people through a six-week program of physical conditioning, general recreation, and career guidance, so that they can return home and be able to cope with the demands of daily living. Almost everywhere, people suffer from worries and tensions and, as a result, they try to find relief in alcohol, cigarettes, food, and drugs of all kinds. Each year, there is more alcohol than gasoline produced in the world. In the United States alone, alcohol consumption is about 11 quarts a year per person. Many believe that this excessive use of alcohol, as well as the huge consumption of drugs, is a response to stress. Here are some of the latest findings on stress:

1. Stress definitely causes some serious physical problems. It can be a contributing factor in headaches, backaches, and ulcers.
2. Stress may be less of a factor in heart disease than was first suspected, although this is still being investigated.
3. Severe stress makes people accident-prone.
4. Urban stress may not be more harmful than rural stress, merely different from it.
5. Some stress *enhances* well-being and can actually be beneficial, whereas a lack of stress can be harmful.

Why is it that some people thrive on stress, whereas others are debilitated by it? The answer may be determined by our own interpretations of what is stressful. Stress does not depend on the external event as such: A situation or event that is stressful to one person may not be to another. Furthermore, the stress itself is a *general* reaction. This is what the most noted and respected researcher on stress, Hans Selye, calls the nonspecific response of the body to demands made upon it.

To illustrate the nonspecific nature of stress, Selye uses the following example.* A middle-aged widow comes home from work and sits down to read the evening paper. The doorbell rings, and standing at the door is a military officer with a telegram informing her that her son, who was on reserve duty, has been killed in a plane crash. What is her reaction likely to be? She will show all the physical and psychological signs of stress: Her respiration will increase, her blood pressure will climb, she may perspire, she may be immobilized, and she may not be able to sleep well.

A week later, the woman is at home when the doorbell rings again, and standing at the door is her son. The report of his death was a case of mistaken identity. What is her reaction likely to be? Her respiration will increase, her blood pressure will climb, she may perspire, she may be immobilized, and she may not be able to sleep well.

No one would doubt that those two events at the door were quite different, and yet her stress reaction was *general* in both

---

* *The Stress of Life* (New York: McGraw-Hill, 1956).

situations. Thus, although we might differentiate between good and bad stress—what Selye calls eustress and distress—the body reacts in much the same way in both cases. If you are called into the president's office because of poor managerial performance, you will undoubtedly show signs of stress. On the other hand, if you are called into the office to be congratulated and promoted, you will also show signs of stress. We would all agree that these two situations are completely different, yet the body reacts as though they were the same. The difference between good and bad stress may lie in their long-term effects.

Selye discusses the long-term effects of stress in his three-stage theory known as the *General Adaptation Syndrome*. The stages are:

Alarm Reaction. This is the first phase of stress reaction. The body summons all its powers to meet the danger or to escape it. This is also known as the "fight-or-flight" response. If the stress is mild and short-term, the alarm reaction gives way to normal functioning. If not, the person enters the second stage.

Resistance. The outward signs of stress disappear. Internally, however, the person is still reacting to the stress. Bodily organs and functions will be affected, but the person is still able to cope with responsibilities. Many managers operate at this stage for years.

Exhaustion. With continued stress, the person is no longer able to maintain resistance. The external appearance of adjustment breaks down, and what is essentially a return to the alarm stage takes place. This is sometimes diagnosed as nervous exhaustion. The person is not crazy, but simply needs to be separated from the source of stress.

As a manager, you should be particularly aware of the resistance stage. If you are alert to this phase, you will notice signs of stress even though attempts are being made by someone to cope. From what we know about stress, both *intensity* and *duration* are related to resistance and to how well a person's stress threshold is maintained.

Thomas Holms and Richard Rahe have developed a numerical scale based on stress intensity and duration.* They refer to events as Life Change Units (LCUs), and their scale has been tested cross-culturally on large numbers of people. On the basis of these LCUs, the authors have devised a Social Readjustment Scale listing 43 major stressful events. Here are the ten most stressful events and their LCU values.

Event	LCU
Death of spouse	100
Divorce	73
Marital separation	65
Jail term	63
Death of close family member	63
Personal injury or illness	53
Marriage	50
Fired from job	47
Marital reconciliation	45
Retirement	45

Their work suggests that these LCU scores might be used as an objective measurement for both predicting severe stress and recognizing the limits of the resistance stage. They believe that various life events that take place in a given year have a cumulative effect. Thus if a divorce and the loss of a job were to occur within a six-month period, it would mean an LCU or stress factor of 120. Holms and Rahe estimate a mild stress to be between 150–199 LCUs per year; moderate stress, about 200–299 LCUs; and major stress, over 300. Interestingly, when they compared LCU totals with medical histories, they found that changes in health were related to overall LCU levels. In the "mild" group, 37 percent underwent appreciable health changes. Among the moderates, the figure was 51 percent, and in severely stressed individuals, it was 79 percent, or four out of five persons, who fell ill during the following year.

* Ogden Tanner, *Stress* (New York: Time-Life Books, 1975), p. 91.

Here is an example of how this LCU stress rating can affect an employee.

Al Menard was a capable manager in a large international organization that had many offices overseas. In fact, in this company, an assignment abroad was considered a stepping-stone to senior management.

One day, Al was called into the president's office. He was apprehensive because he had only been there several times since joining the company. The president asked Al if he was interested in an assistant managerial position in the company's Rome office.

Al was definitely interested. He told the president that he and his wife had considered this possibility, and that they both liked the idea. The president told Al to make the necessary arrangements to go to Rome in about six weeks. The company, of course, would assist him with financial matters and help him arrange schooling for his children. Al was very pleased. He told everyone at work, his wife started making plans, and the whole family was ready to go. Al began to train a replacement for his current position. He had even found a family in Rome that was interested in making a house exchange.

About one week before he was to leave, he got a call from the president's office. When he went in, he expected to get last-minute details of his assignment. Instead, the president told him that the offer had been withdrawn by the board of directors, who apparently felt that Al was qualified, but that it was necessary to hire an Italian for the position. Al was shocked. He told the president that he had made many plans, and that this sudden change would be very embarrassing. The president said that he agreed but that he himself had been overruled by the board. However, he promised that he would consider Al for the next suitable assignment that opened up.

Leaving aside the question of corporate ethics in this case, how much stress was Al subjected to during these five weeks? Here is an estimate, based on Holms and Rahe's LCU scale:

Event	LCU
Business readjustment	39
Change to different line of work	36
Change in responsibilities at work	29
Outstanding personal achievement	28
Wife begins or stops work	26
Change in living conditions	25
Trouble with boss	23
Change in residence	20
Change in number of family get-togethers	15
Total	241

In six weeks, Al has accumulated enough LCUs to be placed in the moderate stress category for an entire year! He may have greater than a 51 percent chance of illness, may experience some depression, and may even quit his job, which could add more LCUs to the total.

One of the most stressful elements of Al's situation is his apparent lack of control over his destiny. This can be a major stress factor in itself, but an early study of stress done with monkeys illustrates how *having* control can also be stressful.

In his so-called "executive monkey" studies, Joseph Brady * set up a controlled experiment with pairs of monkeys. In each pair, the monkeys were restrained and immobilized, except for their hands. Both monkeys could see one another, and they were connected to an apparatus that generated electrical shock. Whenever one monkey received a shock, so did the other. Both were given shocks at 20-second intervals, but only the first monkey could prevent the shocks by pressing a lever. The second monkey had a lever that had no effect on the shock-generating apparatus. In time, one of the monkeys developed severe ulcers and eventually died. Which one do you suppose it was?

You may have guessed that it was the second monkey, because it had no control over the shock, but this was not the case. Apparently the stress of constant vigilance during the

* "Ulcers in 'Executive Monkeys,' " *Scientific American*, Oct. 1958.

sessions had devastating effects on the first monkey. The second monkey eventually became resigned to its fate, whereas the first had some hope of avoiding pain through its own efforts. These results are even more surprising when you consider that studies reveal a lower rate of ulcers in top executives than was previously thought to be. A close examination of the executive monkey study reveals the following: (1) The second monkey is the equivalent of a worker in a job without a great deal of responsibility. (2) The real top executive in this study is not the first monkey, but the person administering the shock—namely, the experimenter. (3) The first monkey is really the equivalent of someone in a middle-management position, and people on that level do show frequent signs of stress.

Stress certainly does affect our personalities and our interpersonal relations. In our interpersonal encounters, it is easy for us to overlook the external factors on what we like to view as stable influences. One point should be clear from this chapter: Personality is anything but constant. The roles, defenses, stages of development, and perceptions of stress that all affect a person are constantly changing. The interactions of these variables help account for the great variety of behavior that is personality.

5

Men & Women

It is no longer possible to ridicule the women's movement. In the United States, women comprise 40 percent of the labor force. Sixty percent of working women are married, and two out of five are mothers. Fully 85 percent of them work because they need the money. Twelve percent of all families are headed by a woman. These figures represent a significant role for working women.

Unfortunately, despite widespread affirmative action programs and the efforts of government agencies and of progressive business leaders, there is still structural discrimination against women in our organizations. But we are also beginning to notice a more subtle kind of discrimination based on ingrained cultural conditioning. This recalls a saying from the days of the Civil Rights Movement: You can legislate against discrimination, but you can't legislate integration.

Structural discrimination is declining very slowly in the workplace. Today, 5 percent of women in jobs labeled descriptively by the Department of Labor as Officials, Managers, and Proprietors earn over $10,000, whereas 95 percent of men in this category earn more than that. Among all the large, publicly owned corporations in traditionally nonfeminine industries, only 15 women in the entire country earn over $150,000! However, there is a considerable lag between when women begin taking advantage of expanded educational opportunities and when they actually become established in a profession. For example, only about 10 percent of American doctors are female, but women comprise 23 percent of all first-year medical students today. Similarly, only 3 percent of the lawyers in the country are women, but they make up 22 percent of the entering class in law school. At least in these professions, it is likely that structural discrimination will become less of a problem in the future.

Many readers, particularly those who consider themselves enlightened and liberal-minded, might be saying to themselves, "Well, I've heard it all before, and I'm aware of differences between men and women, and I feel I'm fairly well informed." Surprisingly, these are often the most dangerous people because they do not understand the subtle cultural influences that affect them. To test your own level of awareness, try this little quiz:

True	False	
___	___	1. Women live longer.
___	___	2. Men breathe faster.
___	___	3. Boys are better at mathematics.
___	___	4. Baby girls smile more than boys.
___	___	5. Women get drunk more easily.
___	___	6. Women's bodies contain more water.
___	___	7. Girls have greater verbal ability.
___	___	8. Men's brains are heavier.
___	___	9. Women's knees are different.
___	___	10. Women use more energy to walk.

At the bottom of the page are the answers. You probably missed at least three. If you did, you get a 70, or a low C. Men have larger bodies, which allow them to breathe more slowly (larger lungs), retain more water (get drunk less quickly), and

1. True   2. False   3. True   4. True   5. True   6. False   7. True   8. True   9. True   10. False

have heavier brains. These are physical differences between average men and average women. Cultural differences encourage boys to be analytical and mathematical. Hence, they are usually less verbal and more active than girls. Baby girls get more smiles from others, and this may account for their reciprocation. Women are more likely to be knock-kneed, but because they have smaller bodies, they need less effort in walking than men do.

Some of these differences may appear trivial, but when combined with our common cultural expectations, they can become significant. Even physical differences can have marked effects. Freud's statement, "Anatomy is destiny," still applies today, although perhaps not in the same way Freud meant it. Today, this destiny is both physical *and* cultural.

MEN AND THEIR ROLES

Since most of the senior management positions are held by men today, and since men are going to be doing most of the promoting, it is entirely appropriate to address ourselves to males and their roles first. Through understanding the cultural and social expectations of masculinity, men may begin to understand femininity and, eventually, equality between the sexes.

There is a long-standing myth that throughout history, the greatest friendships have been those between men. Camaraderie and teamwork are, after all, male qualities, it is argued. However, in his book, *The Male Machine*, Marc Fasteau says that, in fact, friendships between men are usually superficial. He maintains that men are willing to talk about themselves to other men only when they can feel secure that they will not have to compete with these same men in another situation. The effect of this defensiveness, says Fasteau, is to make it almost impossible for one man to get to know another.

According to Fasteau, the qualities that males are taught to value are unwavering toughness and the ability to be in control and to dominate others at all times. The result is that men inject competition into situations in which open interpersonal communication may be more efficacious. Even in casual conversation, this need to dominate is often present. As one man said, "I had to persuade at all times, rather than exchange thoughts and ideas."

These extreme role expectations develop through what Fasteau calls the "either-or" theory of personality. A person who is tough is always tough: You cannot be tough in one situation and tender in another. One executive maintains that independence and other masculine traits are absolutes—either you are independent or you're not. You can't be independent 80 percent of the time and dependent 20 percent of the time and still be independent.

Masculine roles are learned early in life, and sports is one of the most pervasive conditioners in our society, where it doesn't matter whether you win or lose, just so long as you win. Although many more enlightened coaches have decreased the pressure on young athletes to perform, coaches are not the only source of such pressure. Peers, parents, and relatives all contribute, and the effects are easily observed. By watching the two teams at the end of a Little League game, you would be able to tell who had won, even if you didn't know the score: Members of one team will be shaking hands and congratulating each other; those on the other will move very slowly and will not talk much. You can conduct this test almost anywhere—on the tennis, handball, or basketball court, or even in a Monopoly game. Despite some people's efforts to reduce competitiveness in athletics for young people, our basic feelings about sports remain the same.

Furthermore, there is evidence to suggest that the role of sports in character development is highly suspect. As two well-known researchers in the psychology of sport put it:

> We found no empirical support for the tradition that sport builds character. Indeed, there is evidence that athletic competition limits growth in some areas. It seems that the personality of the ideal athlete is not the result of any mold-

ing process, but comes out of the ruthless selection process
that occurs at all levels of sport.*

In our organizations, there are references to sport in such
phrases as "team player," "pick up the ball and let him run
with it," "punt," "hard ball," and so on. Organizations are
filled with grown-up little boys who think they are playing
Little League baseball all over again—only this time the
stakes are higher.

When we look at women and men competing in sports we
get an idea of what to expect in organizational interactions.
Basically the male mentality says that if you beat a woman at a
sport it does not prove anything, but if you lose it is a major
embarrassment. Many men will say that they don't mind losing to a woman who is good at a particular sport, but if you
question them further, you will find out that they always have
an escape clause: Either it is not a sport that requires particularly masculine qualities, or it is not the particular man's spe-
cialty, or he claims that he "doesn't take athletics seriously."
This attitude carries over into social and work settings.

The masculine ideal of toughness becomes part of the work
environment that men design. For some, success on the job is
virtually their entire source of self-esteem. It is not surprising
to men that work is not merely one commitment among others
in their life; rather, it is the center of their existence—not the
job as such, but *work* as a way of life. The common belief is
that getting involved in outside relationships and activities
will dilute the effectiveness of one's work.

Fasteau reports on the ritualistic tests of toughness new
members must be subjected to when they first join organizations. These tests are a measure of the new employees' ability
to "take it." He mentions one bank psychologist who told him
that it is common for new regional managers to fire 25 percent
of the branch managers at random just to demonstrate that they
are tough enough to handle the position. In another case, a top

* Bruce Ogilvie and Thomas Tutko, "Sport: If You Want to Build Character, Try Something Else," *Psychology Today*, Oct. 1971, p. 61.

executive interrupted the chart presentations of a new manager by walking up to the charts and throwing them on the floor, and returning to his seat. The point was to test whether the manager could keep his cool under pressure.

MEN VERSUS WOMEN

Fasteau has a chapter in his book entitled, "The Roots of Misogyny." Misogyny is hatred or distrust of women. Now, at first glance, it may seem that for the majority of men this is simply not true: We don't hate women, we love them. We give our mothers, sisters, and wives anything they want, and we would do anything we could to help them. This is true, but in other, perhaps more subtle ways, we condition young men to regard themselves as superior.

For example, we consider it a phase of normal development if a young girl engages in the activities of a young boy. It is perfectly fine for them to wear sweat shirts, climb trees, and play football. They are so common we have a name for them— tomboys. As adolescence approaches, they outgrow this stage and become "feminine." On the other hand, we *never, never* encourage young boys to act like young girls. In fact, it is a terrible insult for one young boy to say to another that he "acts like a girl," or throws a baseball "like a girl." We have a pejorative name for boys who act like girls—sissies.

Men constantly seem to have to reaffirm their own masculinity. For example, some men join clubs that physically exclude women. Many of these clubs are religious or community-minded, and they provide valuable help to the needy and the handicapped, but they also are a bit adolescent at times. Some clubs have their own hats, badges, jackets, and special songs. One rationale behind excluding women from these all-male organizations is that wives would object to their husbands spending a social evening alone in a coed setting. Another is that men wouldn't be themselves if women were in the club. Doesn't that imply that whenever women are present, men are acting? Perhaps this is true, but what does it say about communication between the sexes? It seems clear that this exclusion process is based on men's need for exclusively male bonding and camaraderie, and on their belief that women are, essentially, inferior. This attitude spills over into business organizations as well.

Socially, there have been some major changes in attitudes about male superiority, but this has only taken place very recently. Five years ago, a study analyzed children's stories for common sexual stereotypes and biases.* After all, many of the cultural attitudes and values of adulthood are based on what people learn during their childhood. In fact, some psychologists say that by the age of three or four, children not only know what masculinity and femininity are, but they already have found their own place on the masculinity/ femininity continuum. In this analysis of 2,760 stories in 134 children's books, there were two and a half times as many stories about boys as about girls. In most cases the boys had all sorts of adventures and interesting encounters, while the girls got most of their thrills from passively watching the boys. These stories suggested 147 career possibilities for boys and only 26 for girls. With this kind of early conditioning, it is not surprising that men don't take women seriously.

This social conditioning and its accompanying attitudes about men and women persist into adulthood. The advertising we are exposed to is much less sexist than it once was, but there is still some sexism in it. For example, one advertisement by a pen manufacturer read, "You might as well give her a gorgeous pen to keep her checkbook unbalanced with." What if she is a C.P.A.? No wonder male-dominated organizations don't like to have female controllers or accountants!

Men also assert their dominance in social settings. Even at sophisticated cocktail parties where all the men and women are successful professionals, the most common behavioral pattern is for the women to listen to the men brag about themselves. Underneath all the social stratagems and subtle dis-

---

* Peter Swerdloff, *Men and Women* (New York: Time-Life Books, 1975).

guises, men's need to control and impress women is still very much with us.

One of the things men hate most is losing an argument to a woman. They will do anything to avoid this. Some use the tactic of the direct attack: Whatever she says, counter it, dispute it, or treat it as unimportant and beside the point. Another tactic a man will often use is to take on the role of the father figure. He becomes a paternalistic advice-giver, saying in effect, "Based on my vast and superior experience and wisdom, I have this to offer you. Take it in humble good faith and go, my child."

For some men, particularly those who are highly competent in their careers and are confident adventure seekers, independent, bright, and beautiful women are a special challenge. This kind of man sees conquest of such a difficult prey as a real test of manhood: it becomes merely the highest form of professional sport. Feminists or career women who are sympathetic to the women's movement are a real threat to these men.

Many male-dominated societies exist throughout the world, and although men don't always have the same roles, their dominant position usually remains unchanged: In societies where men do the fishing and women do the beadwork, fishing is regarded as most important; where women fish and men do beadwork, beadwork is most important. There is no culture in which men have the primary responsibility for raising children, and there is no culture in which political power is primarily a female prerogative. Some would like to see this as a result of natural selection, but it is more likely because of male physical dominance and the threat of violence.

In a less developed society, if a woman doesn't agree with a man and if the issue is important enough, the man can always resort to violence after all negotiations and reasoning breaks down. In those societies violence and the threat of violence is very real. In our society it is both real and subtle. (Wife beating, for example, is far more common than we would like to admit.) When a man gets into an argument with a woman, he may not actually threaten her, but he may remind her of his *potential* for violence simply by raising his voice. When a man raises his voice, it is very different from when a woman does, because his potential for violence is much greater.

These factors also help set the tone for interactions between men and women in business organizations today. Participation in work has been the center of men's sense of superiority and dominance. Climbing the organizational ladder to a senior-management position can be a way of showing everyone—and most importantly, yourself—that you are tough enough to make it.

In the work setting, men often depreciate the value of the contribution of women by labeling it "women's work" or even by belittling the women themselves. If women are good organizers, they must be compulsive people who are always concerned with "little things"; if a man is a good organizer, he'll probably become a controller or senior accountant. Conversely, a woman who pays little attention to details is called "flighty," but a man who does the same is "creative." Where a man is "diplomatic," a woman is "calculating and conniving." Direct, straightforward thinking from a man indicates a "mind like a steel trap." A woman with the same qualities is a "pushy broad."

SEXUAL CONNOTATIONS

Men's attitudes often make them feel obligated to show sexual interest in every attractive woman they see, whether or not they really want to. No matter how businesslike or professional he is, a man working with a woman may exploit the sexual aspects of the situation. He may not be entirely serious, but he does expect a reciprocal show of ego-enhancing flirtation. Some of this may seem quite harmless, but there are two good reasons why it is not. First, the implication of making a pass at everyone is that one attractive pair of breasts and legs is as good as another. This is dehumanizing. Second, there is a fine line between flirting and sexual harassment, and many men never realize when they are stepping over that line.

A headwaiter grabs a waitress's rear, or a policeman makes

a pass at a woman cop who shares a patrol car, or an executive makes vulgar remarks to his female staff about their breasts: These experiences may sound like cartoons in men's magazines, but women are no longer laughing. Women who are victims of sexual harassment on the job can suffer depression, symptoms of physical stress, and job performance problems. If a woman complains, the old double standard prevails: the man is reprimanded, and the woman is fired or transferred.

If this is a real problem, why haven't we heard more about it? Again, socially conditioned role expectations tell us that "boys will be boys." Many women feel that, because of cultural conditioning, *they* are somehow at fault when they are subjected to unwanted sexual advances. As a result, they rarely tell friends, husbands, or co-workers when it happens.

Just what is sexual harassment? In a booklet published by Working Women United Institute (a women's group designed to help victims of sexual harassment) it is defined this way:

> Any repeated and unwanted sexual comments, looks, suggestions or physical contact that you find objectionable or offensive and that causes you discomfort on your job.

In one of its surveys of working women, this organization found that 70 percent of the women questioned had experienced sexual harassment at least once. Job level does not seem to be a factor—female factory workers and executives all report incidents. All across the country, women are beginning to share "war stories." Nevertheless, many women still think that it only happens to them. Women who work alone in a one-man office are in the worst situation, but sexual harassment occurs in organizations of all sizes. Age is no protection, either—it happens to teenagers and women over 50 alike.

Often women's reactions in sexual harassment cases are similar to that of rape victims: They feel angry, guilty, and defeated. Witnesses to the incident will rarely testify, and it's often impossible for the woman to prove that it even happened. If she is lucky, her word will be disregarded; if she isn't so lucky, her moral character and past sexual experiences will be scrutinized, criticized, and ridiculed. When the "old boy network" closes in, women have a hard time protecting their integrity or their jobs.

Although some court decisions have recently ruled in favor of women in these situations, it is still unclear what the legal rights of women are. (For example, under Title VII of the Civil Rights Act, does sexual harassment itself constitute sex discrimination against women, since it can conceivably be directed at men as well—by male homosexual bosses, or even by female bosses?)

How can a woman's work be taken seriously, if she is seen by men solely as a vehicle for sexual pleasure? She has no job security or work satisfaction as long as she is seen as a decorative office ornament. She cannot function as an equal.

OBSTACLES TO ACHIEVING EQUALITY FOR WOMEN IN ORGANIZATIONS

If men are not willing to regard women as equals in organizations, it is partly because women themselves are not yet ready to be equal. Women must overcome numerous obstacles: structural discrimination and male dominance, to be sure—but, most of all, their own social conditioning and attitudes. In the introduction to their best-seller, *The Managerial Woman*, Margaret Henning and Anne Jardim write:

> In order to take advantage of equal opportunity women must believe they are, in fact must be, as competent as their male counterparts. In-depth competence in their chosen field has traditionally been one of women's outstanding strengths, almost an employment characteristic, but competence as a manager requires understanding and skill at working in and with the informal system of relationships in which management jobs are embedded. Such competence represents a stage which most women in organizations have not yet reached, and the guarantee of equal opportunity is empty unless opportunities are created for women to acquire the knowledge and skill which will make it possible for them to understand, to enter and to compete within the informal system of middle management.*

* New York: Doubleday-Anchor Press, 1977, p. xiv.

Women's failure to understand the informal organization of management has deep roots, as does male control and dominance. Henning and Jardim point out that most of the women managers they studied had a short-term view of their jobs and lacked the perspective of a long-range career direction. In contrast, men see their jobs in the context of career advancement and upward mobility. This difference is highly significant.

Why do men have a clear idea of their long-term goals, and women have only a short-term view? From a very early age, men expect to work. In fact, most men cannot remember when they first realized that they would have to support themselves. Girls, on the other hand, are given the message, directly or indirectly, that their primary task is to get someone to support them. In their hopes and dreams about the future, girls generally include a husband who is the breadwinner of the family, even when the wife works. The differences implied by these two sets of expectations are crucial.

Young boys experience many conflicts about their need to be self-sufficient. Can they do this well? they wonder. Are they any good at this? They must test their potential to do something. If not one thing, find something else. They learn to play with kids they don't even like because they need a full outfield or a quarterback. This teaches them to tolerate bosses and co-workers in the interest of expediency later in life. It teaches them teamwork *and* competition. A woman may have different tensions and conflicts. She will need to find one man to support and love her. She needs to be pretty, nice, and competent—but not too competent, since that may challenge and threaten a man.

As evidence of how ingrained these role expectations are for women, researchers investigating the psychology of women several years ago concluded that women fear success. This is quite a reversal of the idea that people have a fear of failure. Fear of success is *not* a wish to fail; it is a wish to avoid success. The desire to fail comes from an unconscious feeling that failure is somehow satisfying. In this situation, however, a state of anxiety is produced by the prospect of success. The question is not what will happen if I fail, but what will happen if I succeed?

According to the stereotype, girls get dumber as they get older. The female matures early, levels off fast, and then backslides. Many are brilliant in grade school, merely bright in high school, and good in college. Why? Because of an avoidance motive. This doesn't tell us what they will *not* do. This is the motive to avoid success. This fear of success is indicative of the tremendous underlying conflict women face today, a conflict between being successful and fulfilled as a person on the one hand and, on the other hand, being the type of woman that a man will find attractive. Psychologists studying women have found the fear of success to be greatest among women of high intelligence who come from homes where achievement was an important value. (This makes sense: The woman who doesn't have a reasonable chance for success will not be frightened by a prospect of success that isn't real.)

Fear of success often causes self-defeating behavior in women. In experimental situations in which women compete against men, the women generally perform less well than in situations where these same women compete against other women. This desire to avoid success often causes women to give up and to deliberately sabotage their own efforts just when they are on the threshold of achievement.

Furthermore, because of these cultural expectations and childhood experiences, women tend to have less political skill than men. *What men learned as boys, women must learn as adults.* Teamwork is a new experience for women and, as a result, they are not as flexible. It is easy for men to develop a comfortable working relationship with their peers; women must consciously work at it. Men can work with people they barely tolerate in a way that women find repressive and hypocritical. Some women often ask why men do this. The reason is quite simple: They do it to win. Why make enemies out of people who may be able to help you achieve your own objectives? Relationships for women, on the other hand, more often tend to be ends in themselves: The quality of the relationship has top priority.

Men understand confrontations and politics enough to know about egos and male pride. Before a meeting, if there is any chance that major conflict will take place, opposing forces will align themselves ahead of time. Or, if the idea is to present a harmonious front, the issues will be "pre-discussed" and the meeting will be as smooth and cooperative as could be. Many times managers who are women are left out of these processes. This occurs either because of male dominance or because the women don't understand enough about informal pressures and counterpressures to give this bargaining much priority.

The probability that women can discard and replace all the effects of their social conditioning is small. However, given my assumptions about behavior (see Chapter 1), I believe that it is possible for them to change—within the perimeters of their past experiences, of course. In this context, a discussion of adapting one's behavioral pattern to the most prevalent styles of organizational behavior is appropriate. I will pay particular attention to how women can fit into these styles.

WOMEN AND FOUR BASIC STYLES OF ORGANIZATIONAL BEHAVIOR

In his book *The Gamesman,** Michael Maccoby discusses various styles of organizational behavior. He suggests that people can be classified as one of four types: *the craftsman, the jungle fighter, the company man,* and *the gamesman.*

Craftsmen are traditionalists. Such people hold basic values about the work ethic and about concern for quality. They enjoy the process of building and creating. They tend to be quiet and mild-mannered. Despite these fine qualities, they can be authoritarian and impatient with other people, whom they view solely in terms of their relationship to the process of doing and creating. Craftsmen usually never make it to senior management ranks, because they value their own interests above teamwork and political maneuvering.

* New York: Simon & Schuster, 1977.

Some corporate research and development scientists are craftsmen, but in a different way from engineers or physical laborers. They tend to be more egocentric and require recognition of their talent, knowledge, and accomplishments. They want and need support from others and, as a result, they seek nonassertive people who will be happy just to share in *their* glory. Unfortunately, many craftsmen, whether scientists or engineering types, don't succeed in management. They often delude themselves about their ability to lead, and, as a result, they may face bitter disappointments in the corporate world of interpersonal relations.

Jungle fighters are power-oriented. They live by the law of the jungle, and believe that winners take all. Defensiveness is their characteristic pattern of response: colleagues are either for them or against them. They are empire builders or wheeler-dealers, but their defensiveness often catches up with them. They are totally unable to be mentors or to develop their own employees, because they are constantly afraid of being overtaken by someone below them.

Company men, or organization men, are people who gain their sense of identity and recognition by being associated with large and powerful organizational structures. They are concerned with the people in the organization, and they attempt to maintain a loyalty to the company. At worst, they are security-minded and tend to be ineffective leaders. At best, they can develop an atmosphere of group cohesiveness and cooperation. They are democratic, but only as long as democracy serves the corporate entity to which they are married. Their company loyalty gives them a secure position in the organization, but it can also cause them to miss opportunities that would help them advance. They may dig themselves into a hole that is secure but difficult to escape.

The gamesman is the modern organizational player. These people are interested in challenge and competition, and they like to be winners. They have a talent for motivating others: To these people, life and work are a game, and their taste for playing the game energizes others as well. They enjoy new ideas, fresh approaches, and neat strategies. They are progressives. They are articulate and witty. They have humor and charm when they need it, and they have a finely tuned sense of appropriateness—they know how and when to act.

Modern corporate managers often combine the qualities of the gamesman and of the company man. They become team leaders. They feel a responsibility for the system, yet they have a clear idea of their personal career goals. They try to find the common ground where what is good for the company coincides with what is good for them. They protect themselves by anticipating problems and solving them before any damage can be done to the company or to their own reputations. They can submerge their egos when doing so will mean a more successful outcome. Their self-discipline can make them excellent mentors.

Although corporations, like societies, need a variety of people and styles to function well, it is questionable how well women can adapt to these organizational styles. At first, women are most likely to be concerned about being craftsmen. Competence is their highest priority because it gives them security. Eventually, they may want to stay in the organization by developing the qualities of the company man. However, neither style will help get them to the top.

Women certainly have the ability to cognitively grasp what the gamesman style means, but the real question is can they adopt it themselves? For men with this style (and not all men have it), it is not only cognitive; it is emotional, it is automatic. This means that they can respond to situations flexibly and quickly. If this style isn't part of your personality, you may be at a competitive disadvantage if you try to use it.

We are not trying to be pessimistic here, we are simply attempting to point out real differences between men and women in organizations. These differences are the result of the lag between new awareness and insights on the one hand and actual change in social roles on the other. The 1960s and early 1970s was a time of important changes in the way we think about male and female roles, but the cultural baggage of the past is still with us. In the 1980s, we must face the problems of attempting to make these new roles part of our lifestyle.

This will not be easy. American men have always had the ideal of the lonely individual who, through independent hard work, accomplishes greater and greater things until he eventually reaches nirvana or immortality. But of course, this is a myth. Another myth is that the American female can, by serving and supporting her man, fulfill her own needs. "Helpmate to man" is a role that too many women have accepted for too long.

We can only hope that in the future, our roles will be shaped by the philosophy that we will not assign specific forms of behavior to men and women. Perhaps we will be able to acknowledge that people can be many things: assertive *and* giving, independent *and* dependent, strong *and* gentle—in short, both masculine and feminine. The rewards are high for both sexes. We could expect such a world to offer a wide range of feelings and experiences for everyone.

6

Nondirective Humanistic Interpersonal Relations

As one psychologist—James Flanders—has said, "Genuine understanding is dependent, above all else, on an eagerness to affirm the integrity of others." * No person has taught and lived this basic philosophy more sincerely than Carl Rogers. It is for this reason that we are using his ideas and principles as our foundation in nondirective humanistic interpersonal relations.

Rogers, currently a resident fellow at the Center for Studies of the Person in La Jolla, California, was born in 1902. His parents were religious and altruistic people, who may have influenced him to choose a career in clinical psychology and to adopt an optimistic approach to human behavior. Rogers is commonly called a humanistic psychologist. Like Dr. Abraham Maslow, Rogers believes that his ideas in humanistic psychology represent a "third force," an alternative to both psychoanalysis and behaviorism, which have a decidedly less optimistic view of human nature. In addition,

* *Practical Psychology*, p. 148.

Rogers has developed an approach called *humanistic phenomenology.* Phenomenology stresses the importance of the individual's immediate conscious experiences, and Rogers maintains that knowledge of a person's individual perceptions is necessary if we want to understand that person. For example, the different people who are changing jobs will behave differently: one may see the change as a challenge, another may regard it as a threat, and a third may view it as an annoyance.

In one of his most widely read books, *On Becoming a Person,** Rogers has a chapter entitled, "This Is Me." In it he lists a number of principles he has learned from literally thousands of hours of therapy and research. Here are some examples:

1. In my relationships with persons I have found that it does not help, in the long run, to act as though I were something that I am not.
2. I find I am more effective when I can listen acceptantly to myself.
3. I have found it of enormous value when I can permit myself to understand another person.
4. The more open I am to the realities in me and in the other person, the less do I find myself wishing to rush in to "fix things."
5. The facts are friendly . . . painful reorganizations are what is known as learning. . . .
6. Life, at its best, is a flowing, changing process in which nothing is fixed.

THE SELF—IDEAL AND REAL

Rogers calls the people he works with "clients" rather than "patients." He believes it emphasizes the person's active, voluntary, and responsible participation, and it also suggests an equality between the persons involved. (This is the same reason why I do not use the word "subordinate" when referring to employees.)

* Carl Rogers, Boston: Houghton Mifflin, 1961, pp. 16–27.

Everyone has a self-concept—an idea of who they are—but no one has a neutral self-concept. All sorts of value judgments, based on our perceptions, feelings, thoughts, and memories of past experiences, are inherent in our view of ourselves. Rogers believes that people have the potential to be constructively aware of their "total experiencing," but to do so requires openness and, especially, encouragement, which may come from significant others such as parents, marriage partners, close friends, and co-workers.

In an encouraging and constructive environment, people develop a change- and growth-oriented attitude, which gives them a positive view of themselves. Unfortunately, not all the experiences affecting us are positive. Parents, peers, and teachers criticize and correct us, and this is often interpreted as rejection. Because of this, we actually develop two concepts of self—an *ideal self* and a *real self.*

The ideal self is composed of all our ideas of what we think we *should* be. This conception of the ideal self develops over many years and in many different environments: at home, at school, or at work. Just as the term implies, some level of perfection is the goal. The real self represents our feelings about the way we *actually* are. The greater the gap between one's ideal and real self, the lower one's self-esteem will be.

Rogers has developed some tests to measure this gap between the ideal and real self. One such test is performed with a special deck of cards, each of which has a different personal trait on its face. First, people are asked to separate the cards that apply to their own behavior from those that do not. The sorting is recorded, and a second sorting is requested, only this time the subjects are asked to separate cards showing traits that they would ideally like to have from those representing traits that they would not like to have. At this point, the differences between the first sorting and the second are measured. The difference is seen as a comparison between what you are and what you would like to be. The greater the difference, the lower the self-esteem. Experimentally, this test has held up quite well.

If you are a manager who has any degree of person sensitivity, you won't need a sorting test to identify people with low self-images. When you do recognize such people, you can be sure that they are not living up to their own ideal expectations of who they should be, and how they should act. When this is the case, all kinds of self-defeating, neurotic behavior can develop. But let us now explore the basic corrective actions Rogers recommends for dealing with self-image problems.

CONDITIONAL AND UNCONDITIONAL POSITIVE REGARD

If there is a significant gap between the ideal and the real self, the question arises, "Do you correct the situation by attempting to move the ideal closer to the real, or the real closer to the ideal?" In order to find the answer to this, we must first examine how the gap originally develops.

A person's self-regard develops from incorporated values based on *other-regard.* It is derived from what we believe others think of us. In turn, people regard themselves positively only when they think, feel, or act in certain ways. This is called *conditional positive regard.* If you do feel this, then you are O.K. If you don't you are not acceptable.

This message of conditional positive regard is not always communicated directly; it is often implied. For example, parents will often hint that their love is contingent on the child's adherence to their standards and ideas. "If you do as we want you to," they seem to say, "then we will love and accept you." Even more conditionally, if the child thinks as they do and shares their values, he or she is even more acceptable to them. This same scene is reenacted daily in school, in social situations, and on the job. The problem is that thoughts, feelings, and actions sanctioned by significant others may be so different from one's own experience and perception—that is, one's own phenomenology—that the resulting inconsistency can lower one's self-esteem, causing one to function in a restricted and self-defeating way.

Much to be preferred is *unconditional positive regard.* This means that all the self-experiences of another person are valued equally and that acceptance of that person is not based on his or her fulfillment of certain conditions. When people are accepted unconditionally, they are allowed a full range of inner experiences. They do not find it necessary to deny or reject any part of their life experiences to gain and keep the positive regard of others. Hence, unconditional positive regard is simply accepting people for what they are—it is accepting the *real* self and wanting to move the ideal self toward the real self. The ideal self is based on conditional positive regard—it demands that certain conditions be met—whereas the real self is based on unconditional acceptance.

You may be surprised to discover how often you inject your own value judgments into a relationship as a condition of acceptability. For example, how many times have you made statements such as these?

"I really like him, but he is always . . ."
"I only wish you were a little more . . ."
"I could get along with her if she wasn't so . . ."
"When you do that, I find you very . . ."
"I like you when you . . ."

In one way or another, all of these statements are conditional. The message is that if you do one thing you are an acceptable person, but that if you do something else you are not. When they don't correspond to the real person, these conditions contribute to tremendous internal pressures and anxieties.

One extremely important point about unconditional positive regard is often misunderstood and misinterpreted: Unconditional positive regard is *not* an absolute, all-or-nothing concept. It is probably impossible to experience complete unconditional positive regard from another person or for another person. It exists to a greater or lesser extent in different interpersonal situations. Furthermore, it should be pointed out that accepting a person does not mean valuing *all* of his or her behavior equally. It is possible to accept others even when we are angered by them. *Within the context of an accepting relationship,* many emotions can be expressed. For example, if a child throws food at the table, writes on the walls, or beats up a younger sibling, it is possible for a parent to express displeasure and anger *without conveying the idea that their overall love and acceptance are at stake!* This is not easy, because we often tend to get angry and threaten to withdraw love, affection, or acceptance when we are displeased with somebody.

This concept has direct relevance for managers. In an accepting environment, it is possible to be critical of *performance* and still have unconditional positive regard for the *person.* Admittedly, this is a fine line, and that is why the overall interpersonal environment or emotional climate is so important: It creates an atmosphere of acceptance in which people can be corrected without thinking they are being attacked.

Effective parents, teachers, and managers have a strong sensitivity to emotional climate. They can challenge and confront people in a psychologically secure context, and at the same time actually *enhance* feelings of confidence and competence. I have often had teachers who were masters of this art. They were very tough in demanding mental discipline and clear articulation of ideas. Around them, I often felt humble and insecure at times but I always felt that they cared for me and respected me as a person. Consequently, later in life, when I was challenged about many of the same issues and I was required to defend my ideas, I was supremely confident.

Often, managers believe that they are acting in a value-free unconditional fashion when actually they are not. We all like to see ourselves as objective mediators of conflict, as if we were all King Solomons. We believe that employees have their own subjective self-interest and conditional regard for one another, but that we, as true ideal leaders, are above it all. Here is an example of one situation in which a manager with that attitude tried to mediate a conflict.

Laurie works in the food service department of a large cafeteria for government employees. She prepares salads, sandwiches, and other cold foods. Recently, her supervisor, Ms. Wiley, spoke to her about being careless in preparation of the food and criticized her for giving portions that were too large. After Ms. Wiley had finished, Laurie walked away without saying anything. Ms. Wiley was upset and offended, and went to see the department manager, Mr. Barnes. This was part of the conversation:

WILEY: I'm having a problem with Laurie.

BARNES: What is it?

WILEY: She works hard, but she is often absent-minded and careless. She won't take criticism, and she seems oblivious to what I say. I asked her about being more careful on portions, and she just walked away. I don't know how I can use her when she acts like that.

BARNES: Do you want to let her go?

WILEY: Well, you know how short we are. Sometimes it's such little things, because she can perform well when she wants to. Maybe it's a personal problem. I thought maybe if you talked to her . . . .

BARNES: O.K., I'll call her in.

The next day, Laurie was in Mr. Barnes' office.

BARNES: Come on in. Sit down and relax a minute.

LAURIE: I know why I'm here. I suppose she told you all about that incident.

BARNES: Ms. Wiley told me her side, but I want to hear what you have to say. We want to be fair here, and I've always done my best to see the worker's point of view.

LAURIE: I know I shouldn't have ignored her, but I'd had enough.

BARNES: You mean, you have trouble taking criticism?

LAURIE: No, but there is a lot of pressure out there, and she doesn't realize it.

BARNES: Is that really fair? I know she appreciates your work.

LAURIE: She doesn't act it, and she picks on such little things.

BARNES: Well, remember, those little things add up. The portions are developed so that we can make a small profit on each item. If you multiply that by the hundreds, when we don't measure properly, we can lose a lot of money. See what I mean?

LAURIE: But I'm not that sloppy.

BARNES: I know. That's my point. Ms. Wiley is trying to correct what amounts to a small bad habit. Do you blame her?

LAURIE: I know that, but she doesn't realize the pressure. She's never worked this station.

BARNES: She did when she was training.

LAURIE: There was no pressure then.

BARNES: I'm not defending her. I just want you to see her side. You weren't very fair to her now, were you?

LAURIE: She just approaches me wrong. I don't know.

At first glance, it may seem as though Barnes was trying to be a good mediator, and he actually did better than some managers would in the situation, but as you read the dialog more carefully, several points should become clearer. First, perhaps Barnes shouldn't have accepted the task in the first place. If his intervention was routine, he was doing Ms. Wiley a disservice by preventing her from working out her own interpersonal conflicts. Second, despite his pretense of getting the "worker's point of view," he had no intention of doing so. He might have convinced himself that he was neutral, but Laurie knew better, and so did Ms. Wiley, or she wouldn't have appealed to a favorable higher court.

Throughout the conversation, not much unconditional positive regard was expressed, nor was there an atmosphere of safety and, as a result, Laurie was as defensive as Mr. Barnes. Because of his attitude, he really learned very little about how Laurie felt, or how she viewed her work problems. Perhaps the worst injustice of all was his pretense that he was accepting when actually he was very judgmental. Basically, if you are judging behavior, don't be hypocritical. Do it, but be prepared to accept the consequences that conditional regard carries—namely, threatened self-esteem and defensiveness.

THE NONDIRECTIVE APPROACH

In this particular approach to interpersonal relations, specific behavior and the power to bring it about is not the immediate objective. The nondirective approach focuses on promoting trust and self-acceptance through unconditional positive regard. Carl Rogers makes this point clear in discussing the rationale behind the nondirective approach:

> If I wanted to look like a smart psychologist, I could go ahead and diagnose and advise and interpret. But if I wanted to be effective in working with people, then I might just as well recognize that this person has the capacity to deal with

> his own problems if I create a climate where he could do it.
> ... I would say my whole effort has been focused on the kind
> of psychological climate that helps the individual to solve
> his problems, to develop, and to grow.*

Of course, in order to create a climate of warmth and acceptance, you must actually *feel* empathy or unconditional regard.
If you unconsciously feel uncomfortable and rejecting, your
attempts to use the nondirective approach will not be successful. It should be noted that I do not expect managers to become geniuses at handling interpersonal relations; it is merely
a question of creating the proper atmosphere and attitude.

In its purest form, the nondirective approach helps other
people get in touch with themselves. We often feel troubled
when we repress our basic feelings and sensations in order to
maintain the positive regard of others. Because even though
we have disowned these feelings and may not accept them,
they are still there and can produce tension and anxiety in us.

Two nondirective therapists summarize this process of
helping another person get in touch with his or her feelings:

> My experience in dealing with many people has convinced
> me that people want very much to think for themselves ...
> they don't want to be given answers.
>
> I try to do three things as a counselor: I try to serve as an
> empathetic eavesdropper who furnishes clarifying ques-
> tions; I try to give information about matters related to the
> problem and try to make available such procedures and
> techniques as I may know; and I accept the person.†

Here is an example of this nondirective approach, although
it must be emphasized that this written transcription lacks
much of the flavor that the original exchange must have had.

* Richard Evans, *Carl Rogers: The Man and His Ideas* (New York, Dutton, 1975), p. 27.
† Wendall Johnson and Dorothy Moeller, *Living With Change* (New York: Harper &
Row, 1972), pp. 181–183.

"I don't know why I'm so sensitive. For example, if my boss says the slightest thing about my work, I feel hurt. I react with a sort of pouting, and maybe I'll even get angry. . . . "

"You have the feeling . . . you feel you're too sensitive about what others say?"

"Yes, why can't I stand up for myself? Why do I make such a big deal out of everything?"

"It hurts . . . you'd like to react differently to criticism. . . . It really bothers you that you can't." *

A great deal has been written about this restatement technique, and much of it is incorrect. Restatement is not merely being a mirror or an echo for another person. Whereas the restatement should be nonjudgmental and unconditional, it should also offer new *opportunities* for insight. By hearing someone else state your feelings even in a slightly different way, you may see parts of yourself at which you had been previously unaware. Rogers himself is explicit about restatement: "If it is simply reflection, that's no good. That's just a technique. It must be a desire to understand empathetically, to really stand in the client's shoes and to see the world from his vantage point."

Another point that is often misunderstood is the idea that the therapist or manager isn't *doing* anything. First, by listening carefully and sensitively and considering that each person has something worthwhile to say, we are confirming their worth. Rogers feels that respectful listening helps create a psychologically safe climate. The therapist is saying, in effect, "If I can listen and accept you and your feelings, why can't you accept yourself?"

Furthermore, the nondirective approach is relatively safe for a manager. The approach emphasizes accepting at face value what a person says, thereby minimizing the danger of speculating about the person's unconscious motives, a task for which the manager is unqualified.

* Evans, *Carl Rogers*, p. 29.

Keep in mind that we are developing a climate, not prescribing a strategy for management action. Thus, nondirective interpersonal relations do not mean a laissez-faire style of management. It is possible to approve, disapprove, guide, or correct specific behavior within this atmosphere and still maintain a positive regard for the person.

At times the desire of a manager to be accepting within an environment of challenge can give the employee a false sense of security, which, when it is eventually shattered, may ultimately cause a precipitous decline in the employee's self-regard. But this is not really the fault of the nondirective approach; rather, it is caused by the misuse of it. If employees develop an unjustified sense of their own competence, then the manager has not allowed these people to think for themselves. Here is an example:

Alan Seidman was a district manager for three small branches of a large electronics firm. As part of his management duties, he routinely visited each branch manager and often discussed personnel problems. About six months ago, he got a request from Pete Petrosino, an employee of the company for about ten years, who asked to take the company-sponsored training course that made an employee eligible for a second-class license. Upon recommendation of Petrosino's supervisor, Seidman approved the request.

Petrosino attended the next training session and performed well, but he failed the exam. Upon returning to work, he was unfriendly to everyone and became moody and sarcastic. He had always been somewhat withdrawn, but now he was almost impossible to work with. After hearing this, Seidman thought he should have a talk with the man.

S: Come on in, Pete. Have a seat. You're not looking too happy today. What are you so down about?

P: I'm not.

S: Oh? Do you always look this way?

P: What do you want to see, a silly grin?

S: Not unless you feel like it.

P: Well, I'm not feeling like it.

S: I'm sorry to hear that.

P: Yeah, well?

S: Well what?

P: You wanted to see me, right?

S: Yes, I thought we should talk.

P: I don't have anything to talk about.

S: Is that right? Well, when somebody drags himself around like you, there must be something wrong. What's bothering you?

P: It's my business. I do my job. That's what I'm paid for.

S: Maybe, but when a person isn't getting along with people he works with, he isn't doing his job completely, is he?

P: You mean me? What am I doing wrong now? Have you had complaints about my work?

S: Well, yes and no. You see, your problem is that you're not a very good loser. You made one try and failed.

P: So, you're going to hold that against me. I thought so. Look, that level is for a more experienced person. I tried, but I'm not qualified. You should have seen that.

S: Well, you asked to take the course. Nobody twisted your arm. I know that level isn't a piece of cake, but other people have made it with less qualifications than you. Hell, you already have a third-class rating.

P: It was much harder than I thought. You think I should try again, don't you?

S: Look, what you do is your business, remember? All I know is, we've invested company time and money into someone who missed his first try and seems to have given up. You tell me if you can do it.

P: I suppose I could. Those other guys aren't any smarter than me. I think it was the math, but I might do better this time.

S: As I've said, it's up to you. Of course, we could always try Dave Martin in the course.

P: Oh, no. Not him. Let me try once more. I think I can do it.

S: That's what you said before. I don't know—

P: I can, I know it. You'll see.

S: That's better. It's no disgrace to lose, but to not try is showing you're less than what I would expect.

P: Well, I'm not done, I guess. I just hate to fail, but I'd like another chance.

S: That's why I wanted to talk to you.

P: Yeah, you win.

Let us examine this dialog in detail. First, Seidman assumed a confrontational style, which can be effective for cer-

tain problems, particularly those involving inadequate performance on company policy issues. In this situation, however, we have a performance problem that is based on self-
esteem and conditional regard.

On the surface, Seidman seemed to succeed in building
Petrosino's confidence, but it may be a false sense of security.
Petrosino's self-esteem was not raised through his own insights; instead, he responded to challenge and competition. In
general, this approach does not work well with people who
have low self-images. Most studies have found that competition and confrontation are good motivators only for those who
already have great confidence and self-esteem. For these
people, the challenge is perceived as an incentive rather than
a threat—but not for people like Petrosino.

Apparently, Seidman did not give enough consideration to
what would happen if Petrosino failed the test again. Even
though he stated that it was trying—not winning or losing—
that mattered, it is clear that he expected Petrosino to pass the
exam the second time around and that he would be disappointed if Petrosino failed. In this case, Seidman's positive
regard was clearly conditional.

How could these errors have been avoided? What alternative approach might have been used? Consider what would
have happened if that same conversation between Seidman
and Petrosino had proceeded thusly:

S: Come on in, Pete. Have a seat. How are you today?

P: O.K.

S: Well, let me open by explaining why you're in here. I guess
you're wondering what's so important. Two things, Pete. First,
I'm concerned about you and your feelings on the job, and
second, I'm concerned about your relationship with others
here.

P: What do you mean? I'm not doing my job?

S: No, you're doing your job.

P: So?

S: How do you feel about not passing the second-class test?

P: How do you think I feel? Lousy. I should never have taken that
course.

S: You think you weren't qualified?

P: No, not exactly. I just—

S: You feel pretty let down about not passing? Like you're less of a person?

P: Look, nobody likes to fail. I'm still a person. I'm as good as anybody out there.

S: So, because you didn't pass the test doesn't mean you still can't do your job and aren't as good a person?

P: Right, and besides I could have passed if it wasn't for the math part.

S: So, I've met another person who has trouble with math. I thought I was the only one.

P: You? Come on. You know your electronics.

S: Now I do, but ask my family about what it was like to live with me when I was studying for those licenses.

P: Yeah, I know the feeling.

S: How would you feel about sitting for the test again?

P: I don't know. It just doesn't seem worth it. I have a good job now.

S: You don't want to go through the hassle again?

P: Well, it's not just the hassle. It's—well, the whole business.

S: It's sort of dredging up all that again.

P: Yeah.

S: Would you rather we didn't put you on the list for the exam this next time?

P: Well—I don't know.

S: You might fail again or you might pass. I'm willing to go along with your decision. Whichever way you decide, I will still have the same respect for you I've always had.

P: I suppose I could try it again.

S: You can let me know in a day or two.

P: O.K.

Here, in order to facilitate an open interchange, Seidman made a real effort to appear as a real person. He took Petrosino into his confidence; he even revealed some unflattering things about himself. He was very open and honest about his concerns and about the purpose of the meeting. As a result of this conversation, if Petrosino were to decide to take the test, it would be more of a free choice on his part, and his self-esteem might have been somewhat less threatened than it was in the first case, because here Seidman seemed consciously to refrain from using conditional regard as a means of getting Petrosino to take the test again.

Seidman did not bring up the second issue—Petrosino's relationship with others. Seidman has two options in dealing with this problem: He can address it at the end of the conversation about the test, or he can drop it for the time being. If he chooses the second option, it may be because he feels that Petrosino's interpersonal problem is a result of his fear of failing the test, and that once this fear is resolved, the interpersonal problem will take care of itself. In any event, Seidman has not precluded raising this issue at a later date if it should be necessary.

INTIMACY AND SELF-DISCLOSURE

This second conversation gives us the opportunity to discuss the issue of intimacy. Managers should learn how to become sensitive to different levels of intimacy and how they affect people's defenses and anxieties. To know when to reduce the level of intimacy and when to increase it can be crucial in determining how open a person becomes. In one situation, a high level of intimacy will foster open and productive communication; yet in another setting or with different people, that same level of intimacy will cause withdrawal and lack of communication.

Here are some statements typical of people at three different levels of intimacy—low, medium, and high.

LOW INTIMACY:

"Right now I'm in the process of collecting handwriting samples as a hobby. It's really very fascinating."

MEDIUM INTIMACY:

"Lately I've been thinking about my relationships with other people at work. I've made several good friends during the past couple of years, but I still feel lonely a lot of the time around here."

HIGH INTIMACY:

"You know, I've been thinking about how I really feel about myself. I think that I'm pretty well-adjusted, but I occasionally feel very inadequate in my job. Sometimes I feel insecure and overwhelmed, just like I did as a little kid when I couldn't do something my parents expected me to do well."

Because of the prevalent survival-of-the-fittest ethos, organizational life often promotes low intimacy. Chester Burger, a New York management consultant, tells the story of a successful company vice president who was rising rapidly and yet for some reason was anxious about himself and his future. When he revealed this to a colleague who was a junior vice president, his colleague's image of him as a confident, invulnerable vice president was destroyed. At that point, sensing the soft spots, the colleague moved in for the kill: He set out to get the vice president's job, and he did. Burger concludes: "If you're not sure whether to say something, don't. Share your anxieties with your wife, or a personal friend, but never, never, to a competitive colleague on the job." *

For this reason, people become very good actors on the job. Although they give the *appearance* of high intimacy, they actually operate on a low level of intimacy. They may come across as warm and friendly; they may seem open and supportive, yet you can know them for twenty years and not really know them at all. There are probably many people with whom you have worked for years, but whose homes you have never visited!

Notice that as we move down the three levels of intimacy, the statements become more personal and the content changes from preoccupation with outside interests to basic insecurities about the self. Not revealing your weaknesses to potential enemies is self-protective, but there are instances when moving to a higher level of intimacy may be beneficial to an individual. This can occur in the areas of self-disclosure or other-disclosure.

In his book, *The Transparent Self,* Sidney Jourard discusses the purposes and benefits of self-disclosure from two perspectives: (1) offering a true picture of ourselves to others,

* Quoted in Rafael Steinberg, *Man and the Organization* (New York: Time-Life Books, 1975), p. 49.

and (2) offering a true picture of ourselves to ourselves. This is his approach:

> We conceal and camouflage our true being before others to foster a sense of safety, to protect ourselves against unwanted but expected criticism, hurt, or rejection, but this protection is purchased at a steep price. When we are not truly known to other people in our lives, we are misunderstood. . . . Worse, when we succeed too well in hiding our being from others, we tend to lose touch with our real selves.*

Rejection, competition, and conditional regard discourage self-disclosure and, at least on the job, this doesn't matter most of the time. But what do you do when you are delegating assignments or considering people for promotions, and you have no idea what they are really like as people? How accurate can your information be if it is based on low intimacy and low self-disclosure? Even more to the point, what kind of atmosphere does your work group have? Does it encourage supportive, empathetic listening within the context of performance standards?

When intimacy levels are low, other-disclosure, or direct communication based on trust, does not exist. People are afraid to be direct. They will not speak their minds or tell you their feelings; they will talk to others, or they will gossip. As a result, you may identify these people as nonassertive, smallminded, and definitely not leadership material, whereas in more open environments, these same people may display great potential for leadership.

The following list may help clarify what I mean by otherdisclosure. Situations are ranked from those that are most distant and easiest to discuss, to direct here-and-now interactions in which trust and support exist.

- I tell you how one person felt in the past about another. Neither of them is present.

* New York: Van Nostrand Reinhold, 1971, p. 47.

- I tell you how one person currently feels about another. Again, neither is present.
- I tell you my own past feelings about someone who is not present.
- I tell you my current feelings about someone who is not present.
- I tell you my past feelings about you.
- I tell you my current feelings about you.

There are several important dimensions in this list. First, talking about others implies a less direct form of disclosure if they are not present than if they are. Second, talking about others is not talking about *us;* rather, it is discussing *them,* which is necessarily less direct. Third, talking about the past is less threatening than discussing the present. Finally, talking to a person directly is most intimate on this scale.

As a manager, your ability to determine the appropriate level of intimacy and act accordingly is important in understanding and supervising people. Some managers have an innate ability to do this and, in turn, to make people feel comfortable. Other managers are so out of touch with themselves and with other people that they will never acquire this skill. Then there are those managers in the middle who, with awareness and practice, can become more adept at sensing these levels of intimacy and how they apply to particular people and circumstances.

If the meaning of self-disclosure is still unclear, here are ten questions that deal with the concept in the work setting:

1. What do I find to be the worst pressures and sources of stress in my work?
2. What do I find to be the most routine and mundane aspects of my job?
3. What do I enjoy most, and what gives me the greatest satisfaction in my work?
4. What do I feel are the weaknesses and shortcomings that keep me from performing as well as I'd like to?
5. What do I feel are my strong qualities on the job?
6. Are my contributions at work appreciated by others, such as my supervisor, colleagues, or spouse?

7. What are my objectives, amibitions, and future plans?
8. What are my feelings about the pay and other benefits I get?
9. How do I feel about the career choice I've made?
10. How do I feel about the people I work with?

In asking yourself these questions directly, you may develop a self-disclosure that leads to genuine self-knowledge. In asking these questions of others, in either a direct or an indirect way, you will give them an opportunity for self-disclosure that may lead to more meaningful and intimate interpersonal relations. Of course, self-disclosure by others must be voluntary, or it becomes self-defeating: The sincerity of any disclosure is suspect when given under pressure.

From a practical standpoint, you must assess the value and need of intimacy in enhancing your interpersonal position as a manager. Intimacy for its own sake may be quite unnecessary in maintaining a good relationship with some members of your staff, but in other instances, close encounters are built into the nature of the job. Often people will tell you more than you want to know. This kind of action could be described more as self-exposure than as self-disclosure.

CONCLUSIONS

Creating an atmosphere of support and unconditional regard for people as persons is not an easy job for a manager. The counterpressures are significant—budgets, deadlines, red tape, and lack of time to relate to others. There are days when every manager feels as though what he has given greatly exceeds what he has gotten in return. Having to deal with so many conflicting demands, dependencies, and problems often doesn't leave much room for unconditional positive responses of any kind. Yet, despite all of their responsibilities, managers survive, and even prosper. They do their jobs, and it has been my experience that most of them want to do it better. Nowhere is this desire for managerial improvement greater than in the area of concern for people. That is what nondirective interpersonal relations attempt to enhance—concern for working with others.

Most people agree that the question,
"Why do you eat brown bread?" can
properly be answered with, "Because
I like it." I should like to convince
you, however, that the question,
"Why do you like brown bread?"
frequently ought to be answered
with, "Because I eat it."
                    DARYL BEM *

7

Persuasion & Influence

Before you can develop an effective approach to interpersonal
influence, you must first assess not only your goal, but the
current position of the person you want to influence. To get to
point B, you must first know point A. Without the knowledge
of where best to begin, you may over- or underestimate the
amount of persuasion or influence you will have to exert.

To avoid wasting time and energy, you should understand
certain general principles of behavior and how they apply to
specific individuals in a given situation. In short, you want to
assess a person's *self-perception.* That is point A.

*Self-perception is affected by many influences, but none is
as strong as the person's own behavior, past and present.*
Some theorists believe that attitude, beliefs, and other thought
processes are simply by-products of behavior, which provide a
rationale or justification for action. Leon Festinger's theory of
cognitive dissonance is a well-known example.

The concept of cognitive dissonance maintains that people
tend to think in accordance with the way they have behaved,
and that they will adjust their attitudes to be consistent (con-
sonant) with what they have done in the past, even if this
requires marked distortions of the facts. For example, according to dissonance theory, after you purchase a Ford, you will
look for ways to cognitively (mentally) confirm the wisdom of

* Speech delivered before American Psychiatric Association, 1971.

your decision: You will remember and more easily accept Ford product advertising; you will discount or criticize Chevrolet ads; and, in general, you will shape your beliefs to provide "evidence" that supports your position. This is a special form of rationalizing, and the evidence is that we all do it to varying degrees.

Festinger conceived of cognitive dissonance as an unpleasant feeling that operates very much as a drive. It motivates us to change our opinions in such a way as to restore consistency and thereby reduce dissonance. Sometimes, we will do this in the face of overwhelming evidence that our behavior was inconsistent with the facts at the time of our decision, and we will develop rationalizations such as, "With the benefit of hindsight . . . " or "At the time I made the decision, the situation was quite different."

Efforts to restore consistency can be blatantly obvious or they can be quite subtle. For example, one psychologist investigating this phenomenon performed an experiment in which subjects were persuaded to eat grasshoppers. One group was exposed to an experimenter who was pleasant, relaxed, and friendly in presenting his arguments why the subjects should try these grasshoppers. Another group was exposed to an experimenter who was cold, aggressive, and distant. Each group was then asked to decide whether to try the grasshoppers. Some subjects in each group volunteered. After they had eaten the grasshoppers, the subjects disclosed how much they liked them. Those who had been exposed to the unpleasant experimenter said that they liked the grasshoppers more than those who had had the friendly experimenter. How does cognitive dissonance account for this result?

The people in the first group had a reason to try the grasshoppers—they liked the experimenter. Therefore, they could justify their actions on this basis. But the second group, which had an unpleasant experimenter, could give no such explanation; therefore, in order to make their interpretations of their actions consistent with their actual behavior, they had to convince themselves that they ate the grasshoppers because they tasted good! Of course, this attempt at rationalization wasn't conscious, because if it had been, the subjects would have realized that their liking or disliking the grasshoppers was only determined *after* they had decided to eat them, and that therefore this could not have been the basis for their original decisions!

The findings of this particular experiment are confirmed every day in organizations. Cognitive dissonance theory may account for the tolerance that employees develop for inconsiderate management: If you work for a boss who doesn't treat you so well, then why do you stay? You may convince yourself that you like the job, or the money, or the benefits as a means of bringing your attitudes and thoughts into line with your behavior.

Conversely, you may change your behavior to fit your attitudes, but this is almost impossible to do *after* you have established a set pattern of behavior. *In general, behavior is a more definitive measurement of a person than his or her attitudes.* If you want to evaluate a person, do you consider what they do or what they say? The answer is both, but if one must take precedence, which would you choose? Behavior, of course. If people say one thing and do something else, I have to believe what they do, and not what they say. This is what the message of cognitive dissonance is about: *It is easier to rationalize your behavior than it is to change it.*

The lesson here is a basic one. Whenever you evaluate personality and behavior, never underestimate your ability to deceive yourself. It is also safe to assume that others have the same capacity for self-deception. If you want to assess other people's self-perception, look at what they do and how they behave, and you will probably not be led too far astray.

The theory of cognitive dissonance should clarify the meaning of the quotation at the beginning of this chapter. Our attitudes are often shaped by our behavior and, once those attitudes are brought into line with what we do, we will reject inconsistent ideas or information. This is one reason why people resist change. We all have a consistent body of attitudes based on our past behavior. In order to be assimilated into that body of attitudes, new ideas must be consistent with a person's existing ideas, or else they must be filtered, distorted, or rationalized to fit in. This filtering process is our basic mechanism for maintaining consistency by resolving cognitive dissonance.

If you are ever going to persuade or influence anyone, you must overcome that person's filtration process. One way is to bypass it altogether, but that is a very difficult undertaking. However, there are ways to lower these censoring filters, thereby making people more open and receptive to new ideas.

CHANGING ATTITUDES

As we have seen, it is not easy to change people's attitudes once they have been established. People cling stubbornly, at times almost irrationally, to their beliefs and may reject the most carefully designed attempts at persuasion. Nevertheless, persuasion takes place every day in many different forms, from a lobbyist trying to influence a congressman in Washington to a manager convincing an employee to change work habits.

Social psychologists have done extensive research in an effort to discover what sorts of persuasive approaches are likely to work. One of the most consistent findings concerns the source of the message. Would you be more likely to be convinced that you need only five hours' sleep a night by a Nobel Prize–winning physiologist or by a YMCA director? If you are like most subjects, the famous physiologist would have a better chance of convincing you. The credibility of the source is important here. That is why aspirin commercials often feature nutritionists or biology instructors. It does make sense to take the opinion of an acknowledged expert over someone who may know very little about the subject, but we can often be persuaded by people we like or admire but who know no more about the subject than we do. Thus, we have athletes selling beer or shaving cream and actors or baseball players selling coffee machines on television.

PRINCIPLES OF PERSUASION

What are some specific ways of dealing with resistance to persuasion? Even individuals receptive to change don't want to change too much, too fast, particularly if it's personal change that is being asked of them. Every manager must face this fact in dealing with people in organizations.

In trying to overcome people's resistance to change, you must first get a clear picture of their behavior and attitudes, and then remember to *begin where they are.* That is, *a communication will be received more favorably if you first express some views already held by the group.*

This can reassure people that you do not hold views that would require them to change too much in order to accept your position. This approach can also help bypass some of the initial filtering process. The following conclusions are relevant here:

In time, the effects of a persuasive communication tend to wear off. That is, there is usually a reversion to old ideas and behaviors in the interest of consistency.

Information by itself almost never changes attitudes. A common misconception is that information changes attitudes. A substantial body of research indicates that increasing information is effective in changing attitudes only under very special conditions. One such condition is that the issue being discussed must be new to the listener and have no prior relationship to the individual's established attitudes. It is a rare issue that meets this requirement. New information that contradicts an existing viewpoint is often distorted to fit the person's existing value structure, once again in the interest of consistency.

There will probably be more opinion change in the direction you want if you explicitly state your conclusions than if you let the group draw its own conclusions. If you provide the conclusions, you do not allow the implications of what you are saying to be overlooked or misinterpreted. Also, because of its built-in resistance to change, a group that is allowed to arrive at its own conclusions will probably decide to make fewer changes, and the changes they do make will probably be more in line with the beliefs they already hold.

Sometimes, overcoming resistance to change is like preparing a budget: *The more extreme the opinion change you ask for, the more actual change you are likely to get!* Within limits, it may be advisable to overstate your case.

Resistance to change also increases when people "go public." *Opinions that people make known to others are harder to change than opinions that people hold privately.* This is because once they have told others about their opinions, they have acquired a stake in behaving a certain way and they must back up their commitments with what appears to be a consistent pattern.

The other aspect of resistance to change—namely, the idea that the more personal the change required, the greater the resistance will be—depends on the level of self-esteem a person has. *In general, a person with low self-esteem is easier to persuade than someone with high self-esteem, especially where social approval is involved.* People with high self-esteem tend to resist personal change because they like themselves, and therefore need a good reason to give up what they see as a positive part of their identity. Those with low self-esteem, on the other hand, are more likely to accept personal change because it may offer the hope of improvement. They are also more subject to social influence, since they rely on external acceptance to a greater degree than do people with high self-esteem.

There is no formula for applying these principles of persuasion, because different situations require the use of different principles. For example, suppose you were introducing policy changes that would markedly affect the people in your department. Before initiating these changes, you would be well-advised to ask some of the following questions:

- Will the message wear off in time, and result in a reversion to the old approach?
- What do I have to add to the factual information to make the changes effective?
- How much should I tell them at the outset about the final changes?
- Should I overstate the case to allow for some backsliding?
- Which people have publicly committed themselves to the old

system and have therefore made ego investments that might cause them to resist the changes?
- Which people have a stake in helping bring about involvement that will facilitate the changes?
- Whose self-esteem will be on the line in this situation?

OBEDIENCE TO AUTHORITY

Since the credibility of a source is an important factor in the ability to persuade people, there can be no single source more persuasive than what is perceived to be legitimate authority. Furthermore, the oldest and most direct form of social influence is obedience—doing something because you are told to do it. Taken together, these two elements are unbelievably powerful.

The most famous experimental studies on this subject were conducted by Stanley Milgram, who used a "shock generator" that had an instrument panel with 30 switches, each of which had voltage numbers ranging progressively from 15 to 450 volts.

The subjects for the study were adult volunteers between the ages of 20 and 50 years. They were told that they would be part of a study of the effects of punishment on learning. They were to be the "teachers," the "learners" were to be in the next room. As each teacher looked on, the experimenter strapped the learner into a chair in an adjacent room and attached wires to each wrist. The teacher was then seated in front of the generator, and the two communicated through an intercom.

After reading pairs of words to the learner the teacher was told to read the first word of the pair along with four possible responses. The learner had to indicate the second word of the pair by pressing one of four switches. Each time the learner got an incorrect answer, the teacher was supposed to give a shock as punishment. After each error, the teacher was instructed to increase the voltage.

The learner was in fact a confederate of the experimenter, so he never actually received any shocks, but the teachers (who were the real subjects) were thoroughly convinced that the situation was real. They were given a real shock of 45 volts before the experiment began and were told that that was what they would be administering to learners who got the wrong answers.

As the experiment went on, the learner made frequent errors according to a preplanned schedule. After one teacher had raised the shock level to 300 volts, the learner began to protest and pound on the wall loudly. When the pounding and shouting began, the subjects usually turned to the experimenter for advice on what to do. The experimenter calmly ordered them to continue, often with comments like "Please continue," or "The experiment requires that you go on. Although the shocks may be painful, there is no permanent tissue damage."

Fully 65 percent of the subjects were obedient to the end, giving the learner the maximum shock level of 450 volts. When most people are asked what they would have done in this situation, they confidently answer that at some point they would have refused to continue the shocks. But this is not what actually happened. Some observers feel that the subjects were sadists or weak individuals, but the same results were obtained using students from Yale University. In addition, the results were the same when women were used as subjects.

Just what was it about the situation that compelled Milgram's subjects to keep following orders even when they thought they might be injuring someone? There were no physical limitations: They could have gotten up and walked out—as a few, in fact, did. The answer is *legitimate authority.*

The experimenter was wearing a lab coat, was doing scientific research, and was in charge of the laboratory. Obedience to legitimate authority is deeply ingrained in most of us. If someone were to come up to you on the street and ask you to remove your clothes, you would most likely not comply. However, if a doctor were to ask you the same question in a medical office, you would do it immediately. Similarly, if an employee were to approach you and ask you to see him in his office at three o'clock, you might be "too busy" to comply, but if the company president were to make the same request, you would probably show up at the appointed time.

The implications of this experiment are profound. It can help explain why many Germans committed atrocities in World War II or why some Americans behaved the way they did in Vietnam, such as at My Lai. It can shed light on the conflict between obedience to authority and personal responsibility illustrated by the Watergate affair. If, as in Milgram's study, an unknown experimenter without coercive power can get adults to give shocks to an individual who is apparently in pain, what can a government organization, with its prestige and authority, command a person to do?

However, there is a catch: The key to obedience is not just authority; it is legitimate authority. The reason we do not have total conformity in our society is that what may seem legitimate to one person may not to another. Managers must establish legitimate authority if they are to be successful persuaders. There are a number of ways of establishing legitimacy. For example, it may be based on *competency*—by being so good at what you do that when you suggest something it has credibility. Or, your legitimacy may be *politically based:* You may know so many powerful people that you establish your own legitimacy on the basis of your influence with them. Legitimate power, of course, may also have an organizational or *formal base.* You are influential because of your title and the authority inherent in the office you hold. If you can manage to combine several of these sources of legitimacy, you will have decisively established your right to authority over others.

PERSUASION VERSUS MANIPULATION

In our zeal to achieve objectives and control events, we often are subject to charges of manipulation. As a manager, you must be concerned about this point if you are going to use your power to persuade. People resent and resist what they interpret as an intent to manipulate. For example, *a source's credibility and persuasiveness is reduced when people perceive that the source has something to gain if they agree to do what he has suggested.* This is the strongest variable in determining an intent to manipulate. The less you are regarded as having a vested interest, the more acceptance your ideas are likely to receive. By assuming the mediator role, you can increase your credibility.

The impact of a persuasive appeal is also enhanced by requiring the active, rather than passive, participation of the listener. In this case, cognitive dissonance is on your side if you allow for voluntary participation. If no one forces you to do something, why would you do it unless you really wanted to? Therefore, you are not likely to feel that you have been manipulated. This is not always possible, but when you can get the voluntary cooperation of other people, you should always do so, even if you have the power to act unilaterally. This is one of the most basic psychodynamic rationales for participative management: It fosters commitment and reduces the employees' feelings of being manipulated.

Another principle that will help reduce feelings of manipulation is that when a group disagrees with you or when it is probable that they will hear the other side of an issue from someone else, present both sides of the argument yourself. This can demonstrate to the group that you want to influence them on the strength of your argument, and that you have considered the objections to your position as well.

Although from a philosophical perspective it may seem that any attempt to influence another person is manipulative, this position is quite unrealistic, and leaves us without any way of handling many situations. *Whether influence is manipulative must be determined by the intent, circumstances, and relative strengths of the parties involved.* From a moral and ethical standpoint, we consider attempts to sell drugs in schoolyards a very different form of influence from that exerted by a first-line supervisor trying to convince a manager to allocate more money for overtime pay.

THE LEARNING PROCESS AND INFLUENCE

We know from learning theory that the concept of reinforcement-reward is crucial to the learning process.

Learning experts point out that anticipated consequences, such as rewards, shape behavior. In this context, *shaping* has a very specific meaning. By controlling the administration of consequences—reinforcement and punishment—learning takes on direction. If the person's present behavior is far removed from the desired behavior, then it must be developed gradually and reinforced when it begins to approach the desired behavior.

For instance, if we want to teach a rat to press a bar, we might have to wait a long time before the rat exhibited the behavior even once, because rats do not normally press bars in their natural environment. So, to increase the efficiency of the learning, we provide reinforcement (in the form of food) whenever the rat comes close to the bar, even if it does so accidentally. This reinforcement increases the likelihood that it will approach the bar again. This process of shaping, also called "successive approximations," continues until the desired goal is reached.

Shaping is important because reinforcement alone often fails to change attitudes or behavior if shaping techniques are ignored or if they proceed too rapidly. If, for any reason, people feel that they will never receive the reinforcements offered them because the goals are impossible to achieve, then they will not respond, out of fear of failure. However, this fear can be reduced by using a graduated series of steps, each one reinforced by a suitable reward, thus building upon each success and encouraging people to move on to the next step until they reach the goal.

Although shaping is important to all learning, including the special kind of learning called influence, there is one type of shaping that is of particular concern to us—*shaping without awareness*. It is possible to shape behavior without the person knowing that such conditioning is taking place. This phenomenon is called the Greenspoon Effect.

A very simple experiment can demonstrate this effect. Holding a series of 20 three-by-five-inch cards, the experimenter asks the subject to randomly select one of three words on each card. The three words have different endings—for example, -ing, -ed, -tion. Although the words are different on all 20 cards, the endings are always the same. The experimenter had decided in advance to shape the response of the subject to a particular ending—let's say, -ed. When, by chance, the subject selects an -ed ending, the experimenter gives a slight nod or says "uh huh," but when that ending is not chosen, the experimenter makes no reply. After a number of trials, many subjects begin to respond to this subtle reinforcement by selecting the -ed ending more often.

Interviews after such experiments have revealed that many subjects are not aware that the experimenter was doing anything to influence their responses. But despite their lack of awareness of the deliberate shaping, they still responded to the wishes of the experimenter. The implications of the Greenspoon Effect, of course, go beyond this experiment. We respond to this effect all the time in everyday encounters. As two psychologists point out:

> The world is, in a sense, one large "Skinner Box," or behavior control laboratory. The contents of a man's environment—his parents and friends, his house and clothing, his food and medicines, his tools and appliances—are the mechanics by which his behavior is modified and directed. B. F. Skinner has frequently pointed out how people living together in groups consciously and unconsciously control each other's actions.*

This statement indicates that at times the person doing the shaping may not be aware of what is actually happening. Shaping may occur without either the employee's or the manager's realizing it. In such cases, the results can be disastrous. There is an old management fable, "The Ill-Informed Walrus," that illustrates this perfectly:

> "How's it going down there?" yelled the big walrus from his perch on the highest rock near the shore. He waited for the good word. Down below the smaller walruses conferred hostilely among themselves. Things weren't going well at all, but none of them wanted to break the news to the Old Man. He was the

---

* Lewis Andrews and Marvin Kaslins, *Requiem for Democracy?* (New York: Holt, Rinehart, and Winston, 1971), p. 22.

biggest and wisest walrus in the herd, and he knew his business—but he had such a terrible temper that every walrus in the herd was terrified of him. "What will we tell him?" whispered Basil, the second-ranking walrus. He well remembered how the Old Man had raved and ranted at him the last time the herd caught less than its quota of herring, and he had no desire to go through that experience again. Nevertheless, the walruses noticed for several weeks that the water level in the nearby Arctic bay had been falling constantly, and it had become necessary to travel much farther to catch the dwindling supply of herring. Someone should tell the Old Man; he would probably know what to do. But who? and how? Finally Basil spoke up: "Things are going pretty well, chief," he said. The thought of the receding water line made his heart grow heavy, but he went on: "As a matter of fact, the beach seems to be getting larger."

The Old Man grunted. "Fine, fine," he said. "That will give us a bit more elbow room." He closed his eyes and continued basking in the sun.

The next day brought more trouble. A new herd of walruses moved in down the beach, and with the supply of herring dwindling, this invasion could be dangerous. No one wanted to tell the Old Man, though only he could take steps to meet this new competition.

Reluctantly, Basil approached the big walrus who was still sunning himself on a large rock. After some small talk, he said, "Oh, by the way Chief, a new herd of walruses seems to have moved into our territory." The Old Man's eyes snapped open, and he filled his great lungs in preparation for a mighty bellow. But Basil added quickly, "Of course, we don't anticipate any trouble. They don't look like herring-eaters to me. More likely interested in minnows. And as you know, we don't bother with minnows ourselves."

The Old Man let out the air with a long sigh. "Good, good," he said. "No point in our getting excited over nothing, then, is there?"

Things didn't get any better in the weeks that followed. One day, peering down from a large rock, the Old Man noticed that part of the herd seemed to be missing. Summoning Basil, he grunted peevishly, "What's going on, Basil? Where is everyone?" Poor

Basil didn't have the courage to tell the Old Man that many of the younger walruses were leaving every day to join the new herd. Clearing his throat nervously he said, "Well, Chief, we've been tightening up things a bit. You know, getting rid of some of the dead wood. After all, a herd is only as good as the walruses in it."

"Run a tight ship, I always say," the Old Man grunted. "Glad to hear that all is going so well."

Before long, everyone but Basil had left to join the new herd, and Basil realized that the time had come to tell the Old Man the facts. Terrified but determined, he flopped up to the large rock. "Chief," he said, "I have bad news. The rest of the herd has left you." The Old Walrus was so astonished that he couldn't even work up a good bellow. "Left me?" he cried. "All of them? But why? How could this happen?"

Basil didn't have the heart to tell him, so he merely shrugged helplessly. "I can't understand it," the Old Walrus said. "And just when everything was going so well." *

The moral here is that sometimes your ability to shape and influence can work against you. *What you like to hear isn't always what you need to know.*

* "Fables for Managers," *Management Review*, Oct. 1961, pp. 48–50.

8

General Principles of Interpersonal Relations

One of the most basic and most overlooked ways of getting along with people is the use of *catharsis*. Therapeutically, the term implies the beneficial effect of expressing oneself. In emotional catharsis, a person feels relief after talking out a problem. Freud developed this idea when he was a neurologist and could find no physical reason for the symptoms of many of his patients. After talking with him, they began to express their repressed drives and the accompanying anxieties. Some even showed a spontaneous remission of symptoms. In eventually systematizing this approach into psychoanalysis, Freud became one of the most famous listeners of modern times.

The psychoanalytic philosophy centers on the idea that in time patients will tell you everything you need to know about their problems. The notion is that, directly or indirectly, repressed ideas will come out. I have already mentioned that the defense mechanism of repression prevents drives that are seen as unacceptable from becoming conscious. However, repression is not able to block indirect or symbolic expression of the unconscious. That is the contribution of psychoanalysis.

Although psychoanalytic technique may seem remote from the problems of management, I think there is a connection. Experimentally, when subjects are deprived of eating for a 24-hour period and are then asked to do a simple word association test, what do their responses relate to? Either directly or symbolically, they make numerous references to eating and food, whereas control subjects do not. From this evidence, we can conclude that people's unsatisfied needs will manifest themselves in indirect or symbolic references or, in a more pronounced fashion, in physical symptoms.

Furthermore, psychoanalysis has demonstrated that giving expression to repressed needs can be very therapeutic. The unconscious is much like a pressure cooker: When the pressure becomes excessive, it must be released. If the release can come about through verbalization and growth-enhancing activity, then it may be called therapeutic.

LISTENING CAN BE GOOD FOR YOU

It is impossible for someone else to have a catharsis when you are doing most of the talking. One of the first techniques you must learn is how to listen. As a manager, you should use this approach with a great deal of common sense. First, catharsis is a professional term for the very simple idea, "You'll feel better if you talk about it." Second, for this catharsis to take place, you must be able to listen, and ask occasional open-ended questions that encourage the employee to talk freely. At that point, you may offer an opinion or make a decision, so being a good listener need not imply adopting a laissez-faire attitude or leadership style.

Listening also has pragmatic and even self-serving benefits:

Listening covers your weaknesses. At least initially, you need not show your vulnerability.

Listening gives you time to think and to consider all the information relevant to the particular situation.

Listening can increase the impact of what you say. Offering ideas less frequently can increase the perceived value of your contributions.

Listening is usually less stressful than speaking. Although self-restraint is involved, it is generally easier to listen than to be the center of attention, particularly if the attention is potentially critical.

But if listening is so beneficial for others and for ourselves, why don't we do it more often? Listening has its own disadvantages and limitations as well: *When listening to someone, don't overdo it.* Your listening ability isn't perfect, and it will fail you at times. *Put less emphasis on presenting yourself as a skilled and charming listener and more emphasis on hearing what is being said.* Some people are so concerned about the impression they're making as a listener that they fail to really listen to what the other person is telling them.

Don't refine your listening to the point where you tune out everyday trivialities and small talk. Most of us don't like to listen to clichés, but general conversation does give us time to think, and to feel comfortable with others. If you cannot accept insignificant comments, you may not accept or recognize the important messages when they come along.

ELEMENTS OF GOOD COMMUNICATION

A great deal has been written about communcation and how to make it more effective, but much of this material is difficult to put into practice, and as a result managers still have the same communications problems they have always had. Perhaps the basic premise of communication is that perception determines reality. Determining the intent of any message, and evaluating its nature and likely effect, all depend on perception.

A simple problem illustrates this principle. When a job is assigned, a manager will often ask an employee, "Do you understand what I want done?" The employee invariably answers affirmatively. Based on this exchange, the manager feels that real communication has occurred, although it may not actually have taken place. If we define communication as an exchange of information, then that has certainly happened, but if we define it as mutual understanding, there is room for doubt. Two weeks later the employee submits a report on the delegated task. The manager explodes, "This isn't what I wanted! I thought you said you understood?" The employee did, but what the employee understood and what the manager understood were two different messages. In both cases, perception determined reality.

Here is a fairly typical example of how communication often does not result in mutual understanding, even when deliberate attempts have been made to achieve that kind of understanding: George Smrtic, a regional manager for a paper goods company, was meeting a former colleague, Chuck Hayden, for lunch. As they sat down, Chuck began, "Well, George, how is the old slave driver these days?"

George smiled. "Me? Come on, you know which one of us is the real autocrat!"

"Could be," Chuck replied. "But at least my people aren't quitting on me."

"What do you mean?"

"I got a résumé from one of your people the other day. I thought I should tell you."

"Can you tell me who it was?"

"Her name is Elaine Shutter."

"Elaine? I can't believe it. She's one of my best workers. I just recommended her for a raise, and she could get promoted in another month. She told me she was very happy, and said she liked her job. I don't know what's up."

"Well, if I were you, I'd find out. Somebody is not telling you something."

"Well, thanks. I appreciate the information, and I'll talk to her as soon as I get back."

After lunch, George called Elaine into his office, and decided to ask her about the situation directly.

"Elaine, I accidentally discovered that you have your résumé out for another job. Now, really, it isn't my business, and

I'm not holding anything against you for applying somewhere else, but I thought you were happy here. Why do you want to leave?"

"Well, for the last two months, you've been telling us in the department that the budget was being reduced, and that we would be cutting back. I thought I'd better get on the stick and look around. I don't want to be without a job."

"Elaine, when I said that, I didn't mean *you* were going to lose your job. It's just that we will all have to tighten our belts and streamline the operation."

"But you said that you couldn't guarantee that we wouldn't have to lay off people."

"Well, nobody can guarantee it—"

"I understand what you're saying, but I'm still concerned."

In this situation, George hadn't communicated the message that he thought he had. Elaine gave it a completely different interpretation from the one he had intended. This conversation did clear the air a bit but it still did not assure mutual understanding between them. George should have defined his ideas more clearly. Elaine was obviously sensitive to the job security issue, and George might have given her more reassurance if, in fact, her job was not in jeopardy.

This danger of misinterpretation increases when communication is depersonalized and when there is little opportunity for feedback. Psychologists studying modes of communication have analyzed the time required for pairs of subjects to solve problems using different methods. The results can indicate which methods of communication are most effective. Here is a sample ranking, moving from the fastest method to the slowest:

Voice and handwriting
Voice and typewriting
Voice and video
Voice only
Handwriting and video
Handwriting and typewriting
Typewriting and video
Typewriting or handwriting only

The fastest methods of communication all involve use of the voice. This underlines the communicative importance of interpersonal relations. Again, depersonalization is present in the slower method. Memos impede good communication: You can't ask a memo a question if you don't understand something. The worst example of memo depersonalization is the printed memo that reads, "From the desk of . . ." When a return memo of the same sort arrives, two desks have successfully communicated with one another.

Good communication demands that a manager have the confidence to interact with people. Many managers talk about their open door policy—they say that their door is always open for the staff to come in and talk to them. But another reason for keeping the door open is so that the manager can go *out* and walk around. One manager I know has a sign with the word "Netma" printed on it. He said that this was his most serious management problem: "Netma" stands for "Nobody ever tells me anything." If this is a problem for you, get up and walk out of your office.

James Lavenson, a marketing consultant, says that every manager should have an MBWA degree—this stands for Management By Walking Around. He believes that managers can discover more about their organization and understand what employees from many departments do by actually getting around and seeing them at work. When managers do walk around, they should be particularly aware of three things: first, that their staff understands what it is doing; second, that their staff has the necessary tools to do the job; and third, that they let their staff know that they appreciate what each employee is doing. Walking around gives you the opportunity to ask your people not only if they know what they're doing, but also if what they're doing makes sense to *them*. If it doesn't, then perhaps it doesn't make sense at all, or perhaps they have never been told *why* it makes sense. Lavenson tells an old story which illustrates the advantages of an employee's having a sense of purpose.

In early Egyptian times, a Pharaoh was in the desert one day inspecting the activity of his slaves. He went up to one slave who was cutting stones into blocks, and asked him what he was doing.

"I'm cutting these stones into blocks," the man replied.

The Pharaoh then approached a man who was weaving long strands of rope, and asked him what he was doing.

"I'm weaving strands of rope," said the slave.

The Pharaoh saw a third man who was mixing cement and asked him what he was doing.

"I'm building a pyramid for you," he replied. The man was immediately assigned to the Pharaoh's personal staff.

CONFLICT AND CONFRONTATION

Sometimes the communication process will break down entirely, and as a result, there may be increased conflicts and even confrontations. How you as a manager handle these situations is an important indicator of your abilities to deal with crisis. Conflict has been defined as having the following characteristics:

1. At least two groups or individuals must interact.
2. Mutually exclusive goals or values exist. These may be imagined or real.
3. Interaction is designed to defeat, suppress, or reduce the strength of the other party by gaining a superior power position.

Conflict can arise as a result of a number of predisposed conditions. Ambiguous authority is a major contributor: When role definitions are unclear, opportunities for disagreement increase. Another important contributor is a clash of interests, such as when there is competition for limited resources. Communication barriers in general can also increase conflict. But the most significant factor is whether the particular conflict is personalized or depersonalized. In personalized conflict, an individual's ego and self-esteem are on the line, whereas depersonalized conflict involves a situational approach which tries to separate the person from the problem, so that the conflict can be solved rationally.

Here is an example of how personal conflict can become a confrontation.

I'm the supervisor of a machine shop in a manufacturing plant. About three months ago, I hired a new tool-crib attendant to help Bill, who was already working there. The new attendant, Jim, is black. At first, I thought that Bill and Jim would get along fine. After only a few weeks on the job, Jim suggested an improvement in the checkout system that was a good idea, and we adopted it.

That is when the trouble began. Bill had worked the tool crib for ten years, and he didn't like change. He didn't like the new system, and he told me so. I talked with him at length about fresh viewpoints, new people, and the need for everyone to be open to change. He just shrugged: He must have thought that Jim was trying to show him up.

After a while, some of the other workers started complaining about Jim. They said he was beginning to act like a big shot. I spoke to Jim about the complaints, and he said, "They all resent me—Bill, too—because I'm young, I've got good ideas, and I'm black." I told Jim that I wanted things to run smoothly, and decided not to do anything else, hoping that the conflict would blow over.

About two days after that, I heard a commotion coming from the tool crib. When I got there, some of the men were holding Bill and Jim apart. They had been fighting and were struggling to get at one another again. I promptly ordered them into my office.

"You know, there are definite rules against fighting here," I said to them when we were in my office. "I could throw the book at both of you. Now, what happened?"

In the course of the conversation, it was revealed that Bill had started the fight and had thrown the first punch. I reminded him that he could be laid off for three days and that a letter of reprimand could be put in his personnel file.

He started to get excited again. "Maybe, but Jim lied on his application—the part about previous arrests. I heard him talking on the phone. He's been arrested at least once. Company policy says you can be fired for lying on the application."

"Whether or not I was ever arrested is none of anybody's damn business," snapped Jim. "The EEOC would be mighty upset if they knew you were asking questions like that."

This kind of conflict is the most difficult for a manager to handle. First, it is highly personalized and contains potentially explosive conflicts involving race and self-esteem. Second, it has become a disruptive rather than a competitive conflict. What may have begun as a perceived threat to a person's job security has evolved into a search for revenge and retaliation. In this case, perhaps the manager let it go too far. Minimizing a conflict or trying to deny that it exists may actually cause it to escalate into a serious confrontation.

At this point open dialog may be helpful, but it may not be enough: Concrete action must take priority over the use of interpersonal techniques. Two issues must be resolved immediately—what to do about the fight, and what to do about the application problem. One of the men should also be transferred or fired, although transfer is preferable in this case.

Here are some simple guidelines for avoiding this kind of confrontation from the outset:

1. Be sensitive to people's egos and self-esteem. A good general rule is to praise people in public and criticize them in private.
2. Leave some time to reach your conclusions, but don't let conflict drag on. Don't let complaints build up for long periods of time—it will only increase stress and resentment among employees.
3. Learn the difference between complaining and blaming. This is a fine distinction, but it makes all the difference in conflict resolution. If at all possible, depersonalize the issue: Try to concentrate on *what* is right, not *who* is right.

Confrontation doesn't necessarily mean fistfights. Conflict can also occur among professionals, where it may be more indirect, but is just as competitive. Here is an example:

Bill was the kind of training supervisor that top-level managers dream of. He had worked on the production line for several years before he became interested in human resource management, and he had not lost sight of the problems of workers. During a ten-year period, he had earned a B.A. in education and a master's degree in organization development and, at the same time, had worked his way up in the company's training unit.

During these ten years, the company's training programs were improved and upgraded to the point at which they were recognized as some of the best in the industry. Much of the credit for the quality of the programs belonged to Bill, who, in addition to his dedication and obvious ability, had a sincere interest in people. Thus, he had been extremely successful in challenging and developing his own trainers, many of whom had themselves been promoted to higher positions. Bill's reaction was somewhat like a proud parent's: He was genuinely pleased that his coaching had helped others realize their own potential. He never seemed jealous when others outdistanced him.

Susan was another outstanding trainer. She had come to Bill's training unit from the production line, where she had advanced about twice as fast as most of the others. During his first talk with Susan, Bill was amazed to learn that she had a B.S. in business administration. She explained that she had taken the line job simply to get employment but that she hoped to advance to a management position. Bill assured her that the company was eager to see each employee develop his or her full potential and advance accordingly. Within two years, under Bill's tutelage, Susan had moved up several grades to become an excellent leader of discussion groups on nearly all aspects of management.

But Susan's success created problems for Bill. Several times, because of Susan's failure to give him certain informaion, Bill was unprepared during management meetings and had to admit his ignorance. Susan, on the other hand, had studied the data she had withheld from Bill and made an impressive showing at those same meetings. The first few times this happened, Bill excused it as unfortunate but unintentional. But when it continued—even after he told Susan to make sure to give him complete reports—he began to suspect that she was deliberately stepping on him to get ahead.

Bill also had a hunch that Susan was, at least occasionally, disregarding the procedures that he had established for the unit. However, he had no proof that Susan was actually undercutting him and his rightful authority. He didn't want to act precipitately, but at the same time he felt that if his suspicions were correct, something should be done to rectify the situation.

Bill should pick the right time and place and confront Susan before the situation deteriorates any further. He should be constructive but honest. By not confronting Susan with his suspicions, he is allowing the problem to fester and is causing himself unnecessary anxiety.

THE RATIONAL MIND

Often when interpersonal relations are discussed, emotional and gut-level interactions between people receive a great deal of attention. This is as it should be, since most of us know least about that part of our personality. But this concern can preclude us from properly understanding how the more rational aspects of our personality function, particularly those whose operations are subtle and not always apparent at first glance.

One rational process of which we are often not aware is a psychological phenomenon called counterarguing. When someone communicates to us a message with which we disagree, it is not always possible or proper for us to say that that person is wrong, so we tell *ourselves* what is wrong with the idea. This is counterarguing, and it occurs silently, without the other person knowing that we are doing it. It is a filtering device when it occurs before the argument has been heard to the end.

Most people who disagree with us are likely to engage in counterarguing. If you are talking to college students about increased tuition, or discussing layoffs with union officials, you can be sure that they will counterargue. However, there are some ways of anticipating counterarguing, and thereby of reducing its effect. By anticipating the likely arguments of your audience, and by meeting their objections head-on, you can defuse their internal processes of argument and hostility, particularly if you are genuinely empathetic with their situation.

While counterarguing is important in dealing with others, it may also be important in dealing with ourselves: We may counterargue with ourselves and not even realize it. This is one part of our rational mind that interferes with our natural desire to process new information.

In his book, *The Inner Game of Tennis,** Timothy Gallwey discusses how counterarguing with ourselves interferes with the learning process:

The Usual Way of Learning	The Inner Game Way of Learning
1. Criticize or judge past behavior.	1. Nonjudgmentally observe existing behavior.
2. Tell yourself to change, instructing with word commands repeatedly.	2. Ask yourself to change, programming with image and feel.
3. Try hard; make yourself do it right.	3. Let it happen.
4. Critical judgment about results leading to repetition of process.	4. No judgment, calm observation of the results leading to continuing observation of process until behavior is automatic.

Gallwey's approach emphasizes the natural aspects of learning. He tries to submerge the counterarguing self long enough for learning to take place. An ideal organizational climate should do the same.

Even though people are basically rational, their thinking can be modified and manipulated by others or by themselves. For example, a psychologist named John Platt † has developed two designs that indicate what he calls social traps and social fences.

Social traps offer short-term rewards that lead to long-term

* New York: Random House, 1974, pp. 82–83.
† "Social Traps," *American Psychologist*, 1973, pp. 28, 641–651.

Figure 2. Social traps.

Time

punishment (see Figure 2). Overlooking conflict is a social trap. Attacking and winning in an argument with your boss in front of others is a big social trap—you may win now, but you're certain to lose later. Social traps have similar effects to those of burning bridges behind us: Although we may understand the potentially harmful long-term effects of the behavior, we do it anyway, because we have a greater need for the immediate gratification that will result.

Social fences (see Figure 3) operate in the opposite manner—they offer short-term punishments but long-term rewards. Not completing one's education is a social fence, as is a supervisor's failure to appraise the performance of his or her people. Social fences often represent an unwillingness to sacrifice now in order to achieve potential benefits in the future.

Both social traps and social fences indicate a lack of foresight, which may result either from a preoccupation with

Figure 3. Social fences.

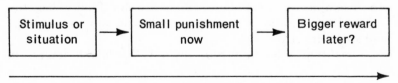

Time

the here-and-now, or from a basic insecurity about the future. In both cases, people behave in ways that are not in their best interests.

INDIRECT SUGGESTION

Let's analyze the following script:

SCENE I

SETTING: *A psychologist is seated at a desk. There is a knock on the door.*

PSYCHOLOGIST: "Come in." *A male student enters.* "Sit down, please. I'm going to read you a set of instructions. I am not permitted to say anything that is not in the instructions, nor can I answer any questions about this experiment. O.K.? We are developing a test of . . .

SCENE II

SETTING: *Same as Scene I.*

PSYCHOLOGIST: "Come in." *A female student enters.* "Sit down, please." *The psychologist smiles.* "I am going to read you a set of instructions. I am not permitted to say anything that is not in the instructions, nor can I answer any questions about this experiment. O.K.? We are developing a test of . . .

There is only one difference between these two scenes—the psychologist's smile at the female student. Can a smile affect the results of an experiment? Not only *can* it affect the results; it probably *does*. A smile can affect reactions in the laboratory, in a classroom, or on the job. This is the finding of a psychologist named Robert Rothenthal whose research focuses on the self-fulfilling prophecy. His work is so significant to interpersonal relations that I shall discuss it in detail.

There are two aspects to the self-fulfilling prophecy. One is internal, and it results from self-labeling—a person's expectations for his or her own future. The other aspect affects others and it results from an *interaction* between people.

Because of certain environmental conditions, a person's perception of good behavior may actually be altered. If you believe that you are good at something, this idea alone can affect your competence. Furthermore, if you believe that other people are good at something, this will affect your evaluation of them. One ingenious experiment illustrates this well. Some researchers wanted to test this labeling effect at a conference of well-known scientists. They selected an actor who at the time knew nothing about the scientific specialties of the conference members, and they gave him a two-hour crash course. After giving a long and complimentary introduction outlining his background and credentials in this field they sent him out to speak to the group. After his speech, he answered questions. He got a long ovation, and speaker evaluations filled out by people at the conference indicated that they were very impressed.

Interaction effects of the self-fulfilling prophecy are even more dramatic. The most subtle of cues can be a factor. When student experimenters are given rats labeled bright or dull, and are then told to condition the rats to run a maze for a reward, the "bright" rats learn the correct pattern more quickly. Actually, although the experimenters are told that these rats have been selectively bred as maze-bright or maze-dull rats, the rats are randomly assigned. This indicates that the experimenters' expectations play a major role in determining how the rats will eventually perform.

If rats seem brighter when the experimenters' expectations are higher, isn't it possible that children achieve more when their teachers expect them to be brighter? And what about managers who expect employees to perform better? We can answer affirmatively, not out of speculation, but from a number of carefully controlled studies that demonstrate these results again and again.

Again, the subtlety of this influence is the most interesting aspect of the self-fulfilling prophecy. In one study, experimenters were assigned the task of getting subjects to respond to photographs of people's faces. They were given identical instructions to read to their subjects. They were also given identical instructions on how to conduct the experiment, and were specifically cautioned not to deviate from them. Only one difference was introduced: Half the experimenters were told that the photographs they had been given were of people who were generally rated to be successful, whereas the other half were told that their photographs were of unsuccessful people.

The results of the experiment were clear-cut: Experimenters who were given the photos of the "successful" people obtained higher average ratings of success from their subjects than did the experimenters who expected low success ratings from their subjects. In fact, after repeating this experiment with different groups, the experimenter obtained the same results, and discovered that the statistical probability that the results occurred by chance was less than one in a thousand billion.

Although you may not realize it, you act out your prophecies or expectations every day. It's tragic when people are given a negative label, are treated accordingly, and as a result develop a belief in their own inadequacy. Over time, the negative image becomes a self-fulfilling prophecy, and it is a very difficult pattern to reverse. However, by giving the benefit of the doubt to yourself and to others, you will get people to believe in themselves; this frees them to perform to the best of their ability.

9

Mental Health &
Interpersonal Relations

During the course of a month, managers may be required to
write a productivity report, a budget report, a profit report, and
any number of other tangible measures of accountability for
performance, but seldom will they be asked to report on the
number of employees they have counseled, or on the overall
adjustment of their work group. But if they were asked to write
such a report, translating it into tangible measurement would
be difficult, even for good psychotherapists, and impossible
for managers who had no training in therapeutic management.

One could make the case that in order to prevent themselves from functioning as amateur psychiatrists, managers
must know something about behavior disorders. How can they
refer an employee for professional therapy if they don't recognize that a serious problem exists? How can they realize their
own limitations if they don't understand the difference between mild and severe disorders? How can they understand
the healthy personality if they don't know anything about un-
healthy development?

Furthermore, mental health affects the nuts and bolts of
management performance. It is estimated that between 65 and
80 percent of those fired from their jobs are fired for personal

rather than for technical reasons. It is estimated that from 15 to 30 percent of the workforce are seriously handicapped by emotional problems. Personal factors are responsible for 75 percent of industrial accidents. These considerations are reflected on the balance sheet.

WHAT IS NORMAL?

A person comes into work, does a job, leaves, and comes in the next day. You observe this person day to day and I ask, "Is that person normal?" But then you say, "Who am I to judge?" What if that person doesn't get along so well with his or her co-workers? Who are you to judge? What if you cannot delegate certain jobs to this person? Who are you to judge? This is the gray area where private life and organizational life overlap. Not only is the job relevancy issue involved; recognition of disorder is also an important consideration.

Often we hear the comment, "Nobody knows what normal is. What is normal to one person isn't to another. How are we to tell?" This is basically an attempt to be charitable, but it doesn't answer the basic question—"What is normal?"

For this purpose, let us consider normal and abnormal behavior from the standpoint of two classifications: descriptive models and causal models. *To describe something and to give it a label is not an explanation.* If I ask you why certain parts were rejected on a subassembly line and you tell me, "Because they didn't meet the standards," you haven't answered my real question. You have *identified* the problem, but a complete answer requires an explanation of *why* those parts didn't meet the standards. Similarly, if you ask me why some people wash their hands continually and are afraid of dirt, and I answer by telling you, "Because they are neurotic," I really haven't given you an explanation for their behavior—I've only given you a *label* for it. For this reason, we need both to identify a behavior (description) and to attempt to determine why it occurs (cause).

There are basically three descriptive models of normality: the cultural model, the subjective model, and the ideal model.

By the term model, I mean a design or construction of behaviors and attitudes that are followed by a group or society. The *cultural model* is a relative design: The explicit and implied rules for normal behavior are decided by the social and cultural groups to which one belongs. On the basis of past experience, superstition, or factual information, a culture sets up rules of conduct designed to foster its well-being. Deviation from those rules is punished by social criticism, confinement, or legal sanction. In general, the cultural model demands conformity. People behave according to certain norms: they come to work on time, dress a certain way, and are passive or assertive, depending on the social circumstances in which they find themselves and on the social roles they assume. Despite its narrowness, the cultural model is workable—it has served us for many centuries.

The *subjective model* is more liberal and flexible than the cultural model. It uses the criterion of personal reaction. If you feel too much pressure on a certain job, and you think you shouldn't feel that way, then you have not adapted well to the situation. The organization or society does not tell you how to feel in this case. If you feel anxious, depressed, or unhappy, then you fit the subjective model of abnormality.

Although the subjective approach has done a great deal to protect individual rights, it has several drawbacks. First, what if hurting other people or causing trouble for them makes you feel fine? According to a strict interpretation of the subjective model, this would constitute adjustment! Second, some behavior problems are characterized by the person's inability to make rational decisions or even by the individual's lack of touch with reality. In such cases, allowing independent judgment to be a deciding factor might be harmful to the person, and to others as well.

The *ideal model* is perhaps the most demanding of all three approaches. It sets up standards of what we should be. Its justification is that unless we stretch ourselves, we shall never realize our full potential. By giving us images of ideal behavior, it encourages us to aspire to that ideal behavior. The ideal model tells us what a good child is, what a good parent is, and what a good manager should be.

Absolutes can be good frames of reference, but the major problem with the ideal model is that, because of its very idealness, most of us can never measure up to its exacting standards. This may lower our self-esteem unnecessarily. It may also cause us to undervalue people, and the ideals it sets forth may become totally unrealistic in our minds.

Each of these three models has its own advantages and drawbacks. Although no single model is completely satisfactory in identifying normality, all three models together may provide a more complete approach.

THE ROOTS OF ABNORMALITY

We must now make an effort to understand *why* these abnormalities and personality disorders develop. To do this, I shall use four major *causal models:* the medical model, the psychodynamic model, the learning or behavioral model, and the stress model.

The *medical model* considers abnormality to be the result of physical disease or mental illness—with a strong emphasis on the word *illness.* The more prominent causes offered by this model include:

Genetics. Family-risk studies, particularly those investigating twins and adopted children, have indicated that heredity may be an important factor in mental illness. For example, children of schizophrenic mothers who are raised away from their families and those who grow up in their natural families have approximately the same chance of developing schizophrenia. This suggests that the disorder's etiology may be at least partially genetic.

Chemical Imbalance. This involves hormones, nutrition, and chemicals of the nervous system. For example, only a drug called lithium has had any degree of success in treating manic-depressive psychosis. Psychotherapy has been an almost complete failure in curing this disorder.

Organic Disease. This is often the result of intoxications, infection, or toxic conditions. Infections such as malarial fever, influenza, pneumonia, and smallpox can result in temporary, or sometimes even permanent, changes in personality.

The main problem with the medical model is that there are many disorders for which no physical evidence can be found. In addition, the pure medical model ignores psychological and social learning factors.

The *psychodynamic model* maintains that the most significant forces shaping behavior operate at an unconscious level. Most of us are not aware of our most critical motivations or of our most important conflicts and frustrations. These conflicts can produce guilt and anxiety, which are expressed in the form of physical symptoms and emotional disorders. This is primarily a Freudian approach, and it is most often criticized by the opponents of Freudian psychoanalysis, who object to what they consider to be its unconfirmed speculations about the role of the unconscious, and its heavy emphasis on the influence of childhood experiences on present behavior.

The *learning* or *behavioral model* looks at disorder as the result of inappropriate conditioned responses or cognitive (thought) disorders. This model would take into account the socialization process, child-rearing, rewards and punishments, and the conscious processes of modeling and identification. Although some theorists separate the learning and cognitive approaches, I shall consider them together. The following example * of disturbed communication would fit the cognitive disorder model.

DOCTOR: Who invented the airplane?
PATIENT: I do know.
DOCTOR: You mean, you don't know.
PATIENT: I do know.
DOCTOR: You do know.
PATIENT: Yes, I do.
DOCTOR: If you do know, can you tell me?
PATIENT: If I do know, how could I tell you? I could.
DOCTOR: You could tell me.

* J. Laffal and L. Omeen, "Hypotheses of Opposite Speech," *Journal of Abnormal Social Psychology*, Oct. 1959, p. 267.

PATIENT: Yes, because I do know. I do know, I do know, ah, who invented the airplane.

DOCTOR: O.K., if you do know who invented the airplane, tell me who invented the airplane.

PATIENT: I can.

DOCTOR: You can.

PATIENT: I sure could.

The cognitive model would argue that disturbed communication is learned behavior that is simply not appropriate to rational processes. Its major problem is that it doesn't account for physical and unconscious factors.

The *stress model* emphasizes the condition of the body when it is influenced by real or imagined pressures, or what are called stressors. They may be physical (noise, temperature extremes, pain) or psychological (insecurity, feelings of failure, conflict, or unusual demands on the person). This model represents a combination of the other three because physical, unconscious, and learned causes for abnormal behavior can be accommodated.

Once again, no single approach is as inclusive as a combination of all the models would be. But how can knowledge of these models help the manager do his job?

Often the manager is more interested in the descriptive process than in determining the causes of behavior. This may be due to the perceived lack of job relevancy in finding out *why* people are behaving a certain way, but it is more likely related to the limits of management training. The following is an example of a descriptive search.

This letter was received by the personnel manager of a production plant that had 700 employees.

Dear Sir:

When I was first hired, you told me that if I ever had a problem, I should see you. Well, I have a problem, and I've stayed up almost all night thinking about it.

My first day on the job, a lady taught me the process of attaching lead wires to the units. I asked about the incentive rate, and when she told me what it was, it seemed very high. After a few weeks, I developed a system and was working along fine.

One day one of the women came up to me and asked to look at my production sheet. When she saw the figures, she went through the roof. She told me I was too damn efficient, a rate buster. I laughed. That was a mistake, because from then on the trouble started.

Almost no one would talk to me. I was friendless. Those women who were the "bosses" were usually old-timers who were loafers, and had a very high opinion of themselves. This clique was all-powerful over everyone except me, and they hated me for it. The vulgar remarks, the silent treatment; it began to get to me—these stupid little people and their moronic remarks!

So their revenge began to work, and my production began to drop. When I went to my supervisor and told her my troubles, she asked me for the names of those loafers, and I gave them to her. It has always been my belief that if some people don't measure up, they will try to pull everyone else down to their level. I became physically ill from the whole mess and began missing work. This is where the situation rests. What can you do to help me?

Sincerely,

On the basis of this letter, let us make a preliminary subjective evaluation. First, this worker fits our definition of abnormal. Whether this is positive or negative remains to be seen but, according to our descriptive models, she does not fit within the normal range. From a cultural standpoint, her work group labels her as abnormal. From a personal-distress or subjective view, she is unhappy, and she is not an ideal employee. There is, of course, the possibility that she is abnormal because she is actually *better* than those models allow a person to be.

We have very little information about possible causes for this woman's abnormality. There is no evidence of a medical cause. There is evidence for a stressor factor, but is the stress real or imagined? There is conflict and anxiety, and there is inappropriate learning.

We have now completed our first step—preliminary subjective evaluation. The next step is to get some facts, using our models as guidelines. Common sense tells us to talk to other people, such as the supervisor, long-time employees, and the individual herself. But how should one talk to these people? What kinds of questions do you ask? This is why I am using the models as guides.

CULTURAL:	Does her nonconformity stem from her attempt to rise above the average, or is it due to her inability to get along in a work group?
SUBJECTIVE:	Is her unhappiness real? Is this a manipulative or self-depreciating gesture?
IDEAL:	What are your expectations about how she should behave in your organization? Is she abnormal merely because she isn't perfect?
LEARNING:	Has she had these kinds of problems in the past? Is her behavior due to learned patterns?
STRESS:	How much pressure really exists in the production area? What has she actually been subjected to?
PSYCHODYNAMIC:	How are conflict and anxiety affecting her work? How much of it is externally imposed by the work environment?

With this framework, you can now ask meaningful questions, and conduct an investigation in an efficient way. Whatever you decide to do, your approach will at least have some systematic support. These simple guidelines can give a manager just enough confidence in judgment to act effectively.

Keep in mind that you are not a private detective, and you are not Sigmund Freud. You are a manager, and you're trying to get a job done by promoting good interpersonal relations among the workforce.

FRUSTRATION AND CONFLICT

Whatever the source of motivation—biological, psychological, or social—it is absolutely impossible to satisfy a person's entire range of needs. Much of what we desire, at either a conscious or unconscious level, cannot be achieved. The two

Figure 4. The frustration model.

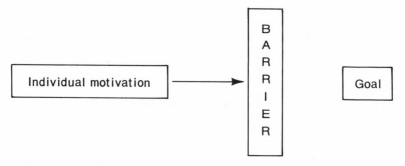

conditions which interfere with total satisfaction are frustration and conflict.

Frustration is the blockage of a goal by a real or imagined barrier. Although certain frustrations are inevitable, most people fortunately learn to decrease their frustrations by recognizing the barriers and attempting to circumvent them, or by substituting more attainable goals. Figure 4 illustrates the basic frustration model.

The frustration model is one approach to explaining how people get depressed. When barriers seem insurmountable, people may simply stop trying and turn the resulting frustrations against themselves. This approach was first tested by a psychologist named Martin Seligman,* who suggested that depression may be the result of *learned helplessness.* This occurs when a person learns that his or her efforts have little effect on removing the barriers to goal attainment.

Seligman originally demonstrated this phenomenon with an experimental group of dogs. The dogs were placed in a harness from which they could not escape, and were given shocks. Later, these dogs were placed in a cage with two compartments and were shocked again, but this time they could escape the shock by jumping over a barrier in the box. A control group of dogs was placed only in the second situation.

* *Helplessness: on Depression, Development, and Death* (San Francisco: W. H. Freeman, 1975).

They had no trouble learning to escape, but the first group that had earlier been given the inescapable shock sat passively, taking the shock without trying to escape. These dogs had learned that they were helpless—that the barrier (harness) was insurmountable—so that even when they *could* escape, their previous experience caused them to create an imaginary barrier for themselves.

Similar results have been obtained in experiments with humans. Seligman points out that depressed people and animals in learned-helplessness situations show common symptoms, including passivity, loss of appetite, and lack of outward assertiveness. *Often these people see no connection between their actions and the outcome of events—thus, the term "learned helplessness."*

In organizations, we are often misled into thinking that if we can develop goals, then we will have achieved a major part of our managerial function. But such a position overlooks the multiple potentials for frustration of goals. Setting goals is only a first step, and those goals must be realistic and attainable. Too many frustrations do not build character; rather, they promote the development of learned helplessness.

Conflict, on the other hand, does not involve the blockage of a single goal. Instead, it develops when a choice must be made between two or more incompatible goals. This is illustrated in Figure 5. In conflict, we see a problem of initially making a choice and then, once it has been made, accepting that choice. This is often because a decision has positive and negative consequences. You may want to fire someone in order to improve the performance of your department, yet the process may be so difficult for you that you may not take action for several months. You may be irritable or overly polite to this

Figure 5. The conflict model.

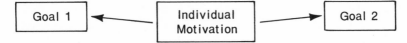

person. You may avoid direct contact or delegate the task of firing this employee for months.

Resolving psychological conflict often depends on weighing the potentially positive and negative consequences of a decision. It also rests with basic fears of failure and of making an irreversible decision.

When frustration and conflict are intense, they may be related to behavioral disorders. Accompanying anxieties are often outward signs that these two factors are disproportionate to the person's goal achievement or decision-making ability. We will see this more clearly in the classifications that follow.

THE FORMS OF NEUROSIS

The word "neurotic" is used widely in everyday conversation. We often say to someone, "You know, you're really neurotic about that." Many times the term is used incorrectly. The professional view is that neurosis represents a behavior problem in which the person responds to life's demands with undue anxiety. Neurosis is either the anxiety itself manifested directly or behavior that represents an attempt to control that anxiety.

Most people labeled neurotic are not hospitalized. They are aware of their problem, although many times they are not able to correct it or fully understand its cause. They are not out of touch with reality, and many neurotics function well in their daily lives. Much neurotic anxiety is the result of frustration and conflict. I shall divide neuroses into several categories for the purpose of highlighting specific reactions.

Anxiety Reactions

When neurotic anxiety is expressed directly, it can take four possible forms:

Free-Floating	*Bound*
Acute	Acute
Chronic	Chronic

The difference between free-floating and bound anxiety is that in the first case the cause is indirect and not attached to the immediate circumstances; bound anxiety has a definite and traceable attachment to an object or situation. Acute anxiety is intense and short term, whereas chronic anxiety is less intense but quite persistent.

The most common type of free-floating acute anxiety is called an *acute anxiety attack*. Its symptoms may include a rapid onset, increased heart rate, sudden perspiration, stomach upset, and hyperventilation. These episodes come on suddenly and occur for no apparent reason. The person is not aware of the cause, and may develop fears of death or insanity. These attacks can occur as infrequently as once or twice a year, or as often as several times a day. They may last five minutes or several hours. They can happen when a person is at home watching television or reading the newspaper, or even when he or she is asleep. Many times these episodes occur at work.

When people are experiencing an acute anxiety attack, they show all the signs of intense fear. They may be immobilized, or they may withdraw unexpectedly from their work station or leave the office temporarily. It is perfectly sound to talk to people who are in this state: You may not get much participation, or they may even tell you they wish to be alone, but in any case, approaching them will not be dangerous to you or to them—they may even want someone to talk to.

In the case of free-floating chronic anxiety, a person is in a state of apprehension that persists for days or weeks. Although not as intense as acute anxiety, chronic anxiety may produce symptoms such as headache, fatigue, and intestinal upsets. Such people often cannot concentrate and cannot keep their minds on their work.

Acute bound anxiety is attached to an object or situation, and is most often seen in the form of phobias. There are all types of phobias. Some of the more common ones are claustrophobia (fear of small or closed places), aichmophobia (fear of pointed objects, such as knives, forks, and needles), agoraphobia (fear of open places), and acrophobia (fear of heights).

Most people deal with their phobias by simply avoiding the object or situation that triggers the phobic reaction. This is the advantage of the disorder's bound quality, but if the phobia is attached to common everyday experience, treatment should be sought for it.

Chronic bound anxiety is attached to a persistent situation, such as work, school, marriage, or family. In this case, the individual is aware of the connection between the situation and the anxiety, but is not able to change it. One may have a job that clearly promotes tension and yet not take corrective action such as quitting.

Many times employees attempt to hide their anxiety reactions. They may avoid doing certain jobs, and give meaningless or evasive excuses as an explanation. They may have a phobia about some part of the task, or they may be in such a state of chronic anxiety that what they were told to do is too demanding for them. As a manager, you should be attuned to these kinds of behavior patterns.

Obsessive-Compulsive Reactions

The person with an obsessive-compulsive neurosis is subjected to unwanted recurring thoughts and actions. An obsession is a thought or idea, and a compulsion is an action or behavior. Although they can occur separately, in most cases the two symptoms are combined.

An obsessive thought may be absurd or meaningless, yet the person may not be able to get rid of it. Many people experience this in a nonneurotic way when a catchy song lyric, a phrase, or a word keeps coming to mind even though they do not want to think about it. Or it may be repeated thoughts of suicide, death, or making money.

Compulsions are obsessions carried into action. People who suffer from compulsions keep repeating certain actions even though they realize there is no sense to it. They are not sure why they do it, and they become uncomfortable when questioned. Some people have compulsions to snap their fingers, tap their feet, or say a word or phrase over and over. For example, a lawyer had to make a small bow whenever he entered a doorway, no matter where it was. He lived this way for many years, and only a few people were aware of it.

One woman developed the idea that there was glass in her food. Before she ate, she sifted through everything. A man found it necessary to wash his hands 30 to 40 times a day, and he wore rubber gloves to keep his hands from being contaminated. Another woman would clean her house continually, washing drapes, waxing the floors, and vacuuming four or five times a week. She even put paper covers on the door handles!

Other forms of obsessive-compulsive reaction are kleptomania (the urge to steal) and pyromania (the urge to set fires). These acts are based on impulse, and it is difficult for people to resist these impulses. When caught in the act, people often maintain that temptation swept over them, and that they tried to resist it, but couldn't.

The following is an example of one of the most common manifestations of obsessive-compulsive reactions a manager will face:

"George, I just got a call from the printers," said Susan, the supervisor of the company's publications department. "They want to know where the proofs are for the new employee handbook. Do you still have them?"

"Yes, Susan," replied George, who was editing the handbook. "I wanted to do a little more work on them at home last week, and I've been making some progress. It shouldn't take much longer."

"I appreciate your desire to do a good job, George, but enough is enough!"

"I know, but I can't be satisfied if I know it isn't right."

"How much time will you need?"

"Oh, just a few more days. Maybe Wednesday."

"That's too long! Those proofs were supposed to be submitted a week ago. We will both be in hot water if we don't move on them. Tomorrow morning at the latest, George! I know I'm pushing you, but it's very expensive to make changes on proofs, and we're under the gun."

When George came in the next morning, Susan was waiting for him.

"Good morning, George. How did you do on the proofs?"

"Well, last night I realized that some of the material in Chapter Three should be in the Appendix. They should be done soon."

"George, the printer is coming at 9:30!"

As this example shows, *perfectionists* often have obsessive-compulsive traits. They overdo everything. They may put in extra hours, but they never seem satisfied with their efforts—there's always something that's not quite right. Perhaps the reason for this is that these people are always acting out their anxiety about failure, and their fear of rejection gets translated into overkill.

Handling such a problem is difficult, because you do not want to discourage these people by reprimanding them for what they perceive as their high standards. Yet their lack of efficient work habits causes them to get bogged down. What you may have to do is create enough pressure by setting strict deadlines so that their anxiety over missing a deadline is greater than the anxiety about failure.

Depression and Its Manifestations

Depression is sometimes called the common cold of mental disorders. It is the most common of the neuroses. It is characterized by sadness, despair, and hopelessness. There are actually three kinds of depression: simple, neurotic, and psychotic. Simple depression refers to mood changes that we all experience for a few days at a time. Neurotic depression lasts longer, and for several weeks this mood can affect our personal and social adjustment. Psychotic depression involves psychomotor retardation or lethargy, extreme hopelessness, and complete loss of appetite.

Among depressed persons we see a high incidence of suicide. Some professionals estimate that from 50,000 to 70,000 suicides each year involve depressed people. There is a debate about whether life events alone bring on depression. For example, one study found that over 50 percent of a group of men and women who had just lost their spouses developed moods of sadness, sleep disorders, and crying; yet only 2 percent required treatment for depression. There are also wide variations in theories on the causes of depression. Some theorists maintain that most depression is exogenous, or externally caused by life events. Others believe that there exists a strong endogenous component based on a genetic or biochemical cause. Interestingly, depression has the most hopeful prognosis of all the neurotic disorders. One estimate is that 75 to 85 percent of depressives get better.

Recognizing depression in employees is not particularly difficult. General lack of motivation may be only one symptom, but it is often accompanied by a lack of interest or excitement about life in general. Marked mood changes from a person's normal disposition may be symptomatic. This overall lack of interest, at least in neurotic depression, will be difficult for an employee to conceal.

Conclusions about Neuroses

There are other classifications of neurotic disorder, such as hypochondria, and more exotic reactions such as anemia, anesthetic reactions, and automatic behavior. I have focused on some of the more common employment-related problems, but the work environment is by no means limited to these symptoms.

In general, neurotic disorders require referral to a professional rather than the use of therapeutic management techniques. A supportive environment will not harm the neurotic, but the manager is definitely *not* qualified to offer primary treatment! This, of course, does not mean that the manager cannot serve as an initial resource person in recognizing some of these problems. It can make the interpersonal aspect of managers' jobs a great deal easier if they can understand the nature of an employee problem, even when they themselves are not qualified to treat it.

THE FORMS OF PSYCHOSIS

If managers are not qualified to offer primary treatment to neurotics, they are even less qualified to treat, or even deal with, psychotic behavior, but again being able to recognize this behavior is very important.

Psychotics can be identified primarily by their break with what we call reality. For our purposes, reality shall be broken down into four basic elements:

PERSON: Do they know who they are?
PLACE: Do they know where they are?
TIME: Do they have a sense of time?
SITUATION: Are they aware of their circumstances?

The psychotic will show a marked problem with one or more of these criteria.

In addition, we can see other symptoms that are usually quite noticeable.

Cognitive disturbances. These are thought disorders in which irrational or incoherent conversation is often accompanied by voice disturbances, such as talking too loud or too softly, or giving words incorrect emphasis and pronunciations.

Affective disturbances. Affective problems are emotional. There may be a complete lack of emotional response, or there may be exaggerated emotional reactions, such as uncontrollable crying or laughter. Aggressive outbursts are common.

Delusions. Psychotics frequently hold beliefs that are improbable or obviously untrue. Although many people who are not psychotic also have such ideas, they do not cling to them as obstinately when given clear evidence to the contrary. Psychotics, however, persist even when shown the sheer impossibility of their beliefs. One man insisted that his arms and legs had been cut off, even though he was standing up. Some common delusions involve power and grandeur. In such cases, the individuals believe that they are powerful or famous people. Persecution is another common delusion—this is referred to as a paranoid reaction.

Hallucinations. These are mistaken sensory perceptions. A psychotic could have hallucinations of any of the five senses, although visual and auditory hallucinations are most common.

Hallucinations can occur in people who are not psychotic as a result of emotional stress, intense anxiety, fevers, and, of course, certain drugs.

It should be clear that these symptoms are representative of severe disorders, and that *the manager has no business attempting to treat them.* Health professionals themselves are often at a loss to deal with such problems, and experts are not sure what causes them. At best, the manager can offer crisis intervention in the work setting until professional help arrives, and little else. However, prompt recognition can be useful to the person exhibiting the symptoms and to the other employees as well. Your prompt action as a manager can be a legitimate part of your leadership role.

ANTISOCIAL PERSONALITIES

This behavior disorder does not involve anxiety, as in the neuroses, or loss of touch with reality, as in the psychoses. For this reason, the antisocial personality is classified independently.

Basically, the antisocial personality shows these traits: (1) inability to feel guilt; (2) inability to profit from experience, special attention, or punishment; (3) inability to form loyal relationships; and (4) impulsiveness.

The antisocial personality is one of the least understood diagnostic categories in the field of psychology. Even experts disagree over what constitutes an antisocial personality. Some writers include alcoholics, drug addicts, and sexual deviates, using the term "antisocial" as a dumping ground for those who cannot be classified any other way.

The antisocial personality has virtually no conscience. This inability to feel guilt and to tell right from wrong means that a major element of social control is missing in these people. Since experience and punishment also have little effect on them, these people are practically incorrigible. They are unable to establish meaningful, trusting, and affectionate relationships. Marriage is a source of narcissism for them, and friends exist only to the extent to which they are useful. Impulsiveness combined with lack of guilt feelings can be a deadly combination. When faced with frustration, these people can become dangerous and violent. They are capable of the most extreme kinds of behavior and can easily disrupt the social equilibrium in the office.

At times, the antisocial personality has a superficial charm and intelligence. This makes them prime candidates to become con artists and impostors. In fact, you may very well have one in your organization and not even realize it. The following is a good illustration of an antisocial personality at work:

> When a man applied to a Brooklyn hospital for a medical internship, he was hired on the basis of copies of degrees from foreign universities. During the next few months, he helped deliver several hundred babies. Over a period of years, he transferred from one hospital to another. Finally, after he had missed a car payment, police discovered that he had never been licensed to practice medicine. At the time he was Senior Resident. . . . The superintendent of the hospital where he was first hired said, "He was a very good doctor." When the self-styled doctor appeared in court, he found the judge had been one of his patients a few weeks before. . . . Nevertheless, he was sent to prison for a year.*

Many social scientists are concerned that antisocial values are becoming more prevalent and that the number of antisocial personalities can be expected to increase. As a manager, you may see antisocial tendencies in employees who don't seem to profit from experience, or who are impulsive and easily frustrated.

These are mild forms of antisocial behavior, but they do not necessarily indicate an antisocial personality in the clinical sense. Managers may be able to detect these traits, but they should be very cautious about prematurely applying that label to an employee.

* George Kisher, *The Disorganized Personality* (New York: McGraw-Hill, 1977), p. 187.

ALCOHOLISM ON THE JOB

An estimated 85 million Americans drink alcohol, and more than 9 million of them are alcoholics. Alcoholism may shorten one's life span by 20 years. Alcohol is blamed for 50 percent of the highway deaths each year. If it's so dangerous, why doesn't everyone just stop drinking? Because alcohol has many so-called "benefits": it can be used as a thirst quencher, a social lubricant, a food, a medicine, an intoxicant, and a symbol of maturity and refinement.

Once you discover that alcohol will increase your self-confidence and ease the pain and tension of everyday life, you will have taken the first step toward alcoholism. The cost in human lives is incalculable. The cost to organizations is enormous—the direct economic costs to industry are estimated at $10 billion per year. Most large organizations sponsor programs for problem drinkers.

What makes a person an alcoholic? It is safe to say that a person becomes an alcoholic when heavy drinking is accompanied by at least three of the following situations:

1. Disapproval by friends and family; marital problems.
2. Job trouble, problems with authorities.
3. Frequent blackouts, withdrawal symptoms.
4. Loss of control over drinking; morning drinking.

The National Institute on Alcohol Abuse and Alcoholism has published two profile analyses on persons with high and low rates of alcohol-related problems.

Highest
Men.
Separated, single, and divorced persons (in that order).
Persons with no religious affiliation.
Persons who drink beer instead of liquor or wine.

Lowest
Women.
Persons over 50.

Widowed or married persons.
Persons of Jewish religious affiliation.
Residents of rural areas.
Residents of the South.
Persons with postgraduate education.
Wine drinkers.

Problem drinkers are problem people. They are not only problems to themselves; they are problems to employers as well. Managers should be aware of their own company programs designed to deal with alcoholics. Expect attempts to deny the problem, to escape it, and to eliminate it through renewed but short-lived efforts at abstinence.

As a manager your ability to recognize an alcoholic is more important than any insecurities you may have about your counseling skills. Even professionals report conflicting or *mixed* results in therapy. Here is a typical example of what a manager might encounter.

The first time it happened was at the going-away party for a retiring employee: Jim, a junior account executive with a New York advertising firm, got drunk. Sam, the account manager, attributed it to the spirit of the occasion.

A few months later, Sam noticed that Jim consistently came back from lunch late. On some afternoons, Jim would be very quiet—sometimes he wouldn't come out of his office. At other times, he would come in laughing and chatting with everyone. On these occasions, Sam thought he smelled alcohol on Jim's breath.

Jim was a bright advertising person. He was extroverted, and was generally well-liked. But recently, his performance had begun to slip, and some clients mentioned that they were not as happy with his handling of their accounts as they had once been.

One afternoon, Sam called Jim into his office to discuss an account. The moment Jim walked in, Sam knew that he had been drinking. As Jim collapsed into the nearest chair, Sam said, "Well, it looks like you've had one too many, Jim."

"Yeah, I know," Jim answered. "I had lunch with B.J. of

Acme Plastics. You know what happens when you refuse to drink with him—he gets really offended."

"Look, Jim," Sam said, "I know that clients like to drink—it's a fact of life in advertising—but you've overdone it. I think it's time you started cutting down, don't you?" Jim agreed, and staggered out.

For the next few months, Jim seemed to have sobered up. He worked hard, stopped taking extended lunches, and his performance improved.

Then, one morning, Sam got a call from the typing room. "Sam," Andrea said, "one of your account people is down here. I think he's drunk, and he's bothering the women. Can you do something?"

Needless to say, it was Jim who was bothering the women. What should Sam do? He should send Jim home and have a serious talk with him the next morning. Part of the problem may have been Sam's earlier reluctance to be more assertive. Basically, Sam should now present Jim with a conditional confrontation: Either Jim accepts referral to the company medical department or to his own medical resources, or he will risk termination in a matter of weeks. Threats of immediate termination may not be necessary or appropriate at this point; a conditional confrontation would be a better first step.

Your ability to recognize and accept the responsibility of confronting an employee is crucial. This is entirely within the scope of your job—do not allow the argument that it is none of your business to deter you! It may be an employee's personal problem, but it is not affecting only that employee's personal life. *Personal problems can become organizational problems,* and once this occurs—like it or not—it's your concern as a manager.

DRUG USE AND ABUSE

Throughout history people have taken various chemical substances to change their moods, perceptual processes, or thoughts. Drugs can alter consciousness in a variety of ways. Depending on the drug, it can cause (1) cognitive disturbances, (2) changes in our sense of time, (3) distortions of perception, and (4) emotional changes.

Drugs that affect consciousness or behavior are called *psychoactive drugs*. Here is a brief quiz to test your knowledge about psychoactive drugs:

1. *Medically* speaking, alcohol (the drink) is (a) useful in inducing sleep (b) important in disease control (c) widely used to relieve pain (d) of little value
2. Someone who has taken more than a safe dosage of an opiate is likely to be (a) excited and active (b) quiet and inactive (c) aggressive and hostile (d) tense and paranoid
3. *Medically* speaking, barbiturates are important for (a) inducing sleep (b) muscle relaxation (c) pain reduction (d) research purposes
4. Physically harmful side effects most often associated with the abuse of minor tranquilizers are (a) kidney damage (b) reproductive organ damage (c) hypertension (d) blood cell damage.
5. By taking amphetamines, people increase their ability to (a) take tests better (b) think more clearly (c) stay awake (d) remain calm under stress
6. *Medically*, hallucinogens are important in (a) pain relief (b) controlling tension (c) reducing depression (d) brain research
7. Teenagers who use psychoactive drugs first try them by getting them from (a) their parents (b) their friends (c) stealing (d) pushers
8. The term "flashback" is usually associated with the drug (a) heroin (b) LSD (c) amphetamines (d) marijuana
9. By abusing which of the following drugs are your chances of brain damage high? (a) marijuana (b) LSD (c) Methedrine (d) heroin
10. Which drug is responsible for the greatest number of deaths from overdose? (a) hallucinogens (b) amphetamines (c) opiates (d) barbiturates

Here are the answers and some explanations:

1. **(d)** Alcohol is not generally considered a medicinal drug, although it may be present in some preparations.
2. **(b)** Opiates have a depressant effect.

3. **(a)** Barbiturates are prescribed as sleeping pills.
4. **(d)** The minor tranquilizers alter cells if abused.
5. **(c)** Amphetamines are stimulants.
6. **(d)** Hallucinogens are used legally only in experimental settings.
7. **(b)** Most young people do *not* first go to their parents' medicine cabinet when they are looking for drugs.
8. **(b)** Hallucinogens such as LSD may produce simulated recurrences.
9. **(c)** Methedrine is an amphetamine that is sometimes called speed.
10. **(d)** Barbiturates are nervous system depressants. If you take enough of them, they can depress and even stop respiration. They are widely available through prescription.

I hope that this little quiz has increased your level of awareness about certain drugs. To increase your general knowledge further, I shall discuss some of the more commonly used drugs and their effects.

The most widely prescribed drug in America, Valium, is the Hoffmann–La Roche brand name for a minor tranquilizer. It is most often indicated for relieving tension and anxiety. Recently, however, it has come under more strict control, because it was being prescribed too casually. Abuse of Valium is serious: Users can develop a tolerance—that is, it takes higher and higher doses of the drug over time to produce the same effect. You can also develop a physiological dependence, particularly when the drug is abused. In other words, *it is addictive.* In fact, untreated withdrawal from overuse can be more difficult than withdrawal from narcotics. These problems do not generally arise with normal use, but abuse does exist, and you should be aware of its effects. Expect lethargic, overly passive behavior and reaction times. Look for a flat, affected voice and frequent loss of attention.

Stimulants, under brand names such as Benzedrine, Dexedrine, or Methedrine, are classified as amphetamines. They increase feelings of alertness, and decrease fatigue. Caffeine and nicotine are minor stimulants. One side effect of using stimulants is decreased appetite. Therefore, in the 1960s, they were widely prescribed as diet pills. Although they are not physically addictive, people can develop a tolerance to them. The most powerful of the stimulants is cocaine, which has become very popular in recent years. Some maintain that in addition to decreasing fatigue it stimulates the sex drive. Cocaine is expensive and is likely to be used by more white-collar than blue-collar employees.

Barbiturates, under brand names such as Nembutal, Seconal, Veronal, and Tuinal, are sedatives—prescription drugs that are used as sleeping pills. There are several problems with their continuous use: First, people can easily develop a tolerance to them; second, they are addictive; and third, recent evidence indicates that barbiturates as well as nonprescription sleeping aids may interfere with dreaming and REM (rapid eye movement) sleep. Some researchers speculate that such interference may affect the vital transmitter chemicals in the brain. One common complaint, which may be related to this, is the morning drug hangover induced by barbiturates.

Cannabis is the generic name for marijuana and hashish. These drugs induce mood changes and affect consciousness. They are *not* addictive, and people don't develop a tolerance to them. In fact, there is some evidence that a reverse tolerance is possible: It takes less and less of the drug over time to produce the same result.

When drugs have so many negative effects, why do people take them? There are many reasons: (1) a feeling of missing out or not being "with it" if they refrain from taking them; (2) a need to prove one's emotional and intellectual maturity; (3) a search for meaning; (4) an escape from feelings of inadequacy; and (5) an effort to develop feelings of closeness with others.

As a manager, you are most likely to encounter three types of drug users: people taking tranquilizers, people taking amphetamines, and those smoking marijuana. Unless a person is on a major tranquilizer or a high dose of minor tranquilizers, you will only notice reduced movement, slowness of thought, and a general slowed reaction. People taking tranquilizers will function on the job. Those on amphetamines will jump from one uncompleted effort to another, seemingly without regard to the quality of their work. They will seem very energetic, but they may be irritable and show personality changes.

You will not notice moderate marijuana users. The most recent studies show that marijuana has little effect on sensory acuity or reaction time. Marijuana may, however, impair performance on complex tasks that require a good judgment of time and those that require a multitude of responses. It will impair driving ability, but less so than alcohol. Marijuana does have an effect on the transmitter chemicals in the brain, but whether these effects are long-term is still being investigated.

In general, drug use requires referral. It is usually a mistake for a manager to alert police authorities rather than medical people within the organization. Once you refer a person to the medical or personnel department, you have discharged your managerial and legal responsibility. Law enforcement involvement can occur through the initiatives of treatment centers: Your reporting a drug user to the police will only complicate your role, and may not be helpful to the affected person.

Much of the information in this chapter may not appear to have immediate value to you as a manager, but during the extended course of your leadership role over the years you may discover that the variety and, quite frankly, the bizarreness of people is amazing. On the job, you will be called upon at some point to confront and deal with many of the problems and classifications listed. I am confident of this from the stories I have heard from many managers.

As a behavioral scientist, I am particularly concerned that you use judgment and discretion in applying this information. A little information may be a dangerous thing, but it is my belief that ignorance is more dangerous. I believe that providing this kind of background on a serious problem facing many workers today is entirely consistent with the concept of therapeutic management which is discussed earlier in this book.

In your managerial role, you should not hesitate to ask behavioral questions of professionals in your organization. This may mean the personnel department, but more likely it will involve the medical department with an M.D. or, if you're fortunate enough to have one, a staff psychologist. Even though you may make referrals for more complex or severe problems, your general knowledge of behavioral disorders will improve your image as a manager skilled in interpersonal relations.

10

Conclusion

Ultimately, interpersonal relations involve complex perceptions, judgments, and actions. In some respects, good interpersonal relations require an attitude: A frame of mind, a set of abilities, and a sense of appropriateness. For some managers, this is a natural response to any life situation. For others, it first requires understanding and awareness and the desire to succeed interpersonally. After that, a demanding process of change must occur.

The naturals—those who relate to others easily and comfortably—must concern themselves with managerial strategy and tactics: They must learn to be gamesmen. Those with insight and motivation who do not have this seemingly automatic ability to relate well to people must concern themselves, at least initially, with reflection on the dynamics of interpersonal encounters down to the smallest detail. These details are the key to change: The "little things" that are so often discounted by managers are often very important to the people involved. Being aware of these details is just another way of being sensitive to the people with whom you are working.

I wish I knew how many times I have said seemingly innocuous things to people who gave my remarks an entirely different meaning from the one I intended. It was only through feedback from third persons or from the individuals themselves much later that I learned how misguided and ill-timed my comments were. But through reflection and careful consideration, I have been able at least to modify my tendency to lose touch with a sense of appropriateness when talking to people.

Paying attention to the appropriateness of what you say does not mean that you as a manager must always be docile or conciliatory; on the contrary, appropriateness sometimes means control and assertiveness. It means being able to determine how best to react to the specific demands of each situation.

If I were asked to offer the single most important guide to good interpersonal relations, it would be this: Don't underestimate the role of emotions. The idea that people are rational beings is only partially correct: They are always rational, except when they are irrational. Economists and philosophers have made assumptions about rationality for years; psychologists have not. It is possible to understand behavior, but that doesn't make the behavior itself rational. Since most managers are well-informed on the rational topics of economic theory, finance, accounting, and strategic planning, they assume that people behave this way.

People often do act in what they perceive to be their own best interest, but whether this is objectively the case in certain situations is often open to question. For example, a manager may want to correct a problem employee through a direct or hard-sell approach. To the manager this may seem rational; however, to the employee, it may seem like a personal insult and, as a result, the employee intentionally cuts back production. The manager thought the action was rational, the employee's reaction was emotional, and the results were not in the best interest of the manager.

Do not underestimate the power of emotion. Emotion is part of our personality. It is a crucial safety valve. Yet, in an organizational setting, emotional control is often required. As a manager, you must control your actions and your anger, even when you may want to explode.

Another common interpersonal problem is that managers

often assume that they must be consistent in their dealings with other people. The need for interpersonal consistency is a myth. Honesty, trust, and straightforwardness are essential, but consistency is not necessarily that important. As two eminent management theorists point out:

> It is not surprising that consistency causes managers to fail, for one cardinal imperative of life as a manager is the necessity to perceive differences—differences between one situation and another, differences between people, circumstances, motives, assumptions, and physical and technological realities. The manager analyzes in order to discern differences.*

This kind of flexibility allows managers to act appropriately in most situations. If we were to analyze the traits of managers, we might place these different characteristics in a continuum. For example, in *personal relationships*, the continuum might look like this:

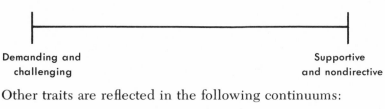

Demanding and   Supportive
challenging   and nondirective

Other traits are reflected in the following continuums:

OPENNESS TO INFLUENCE

Flexible   Persistent, determined,
                                    and single-minded

COGNITIVE STYLE

Inductive   Deductive

* William Skinner and Earl Sasser, "Managers with Impact," *Harvard Business Review,* Nov.–Dec. 1977, p. 143.

ANALYTICAL PATTERNS

Intuitive   Analytical

Movement along these continuums might very well be inconsistent and highly circumstantial. In profiling a managerial style, you might outline 30 or 40 of these traits, all subject to movement along this two-dimensional framework.

This flexible approach to management is essential to good interpersonal relations. Although it is more sophisticated, this managerial style is similar to a variable-ratio schedule of reinforcement, which is effective in conditioning animals. Variability encourages a strong response because of the anticipation of reward. Again, management theory endorses this approach:

> Paradoxically, successful implementors have many styles. They are regularly inconsistent. . . . They get into fine detail in one situation yet stay at the strategic level in another. . . . They communicate verbally with some colleagues and in writing with others. They analyze some problems in great depth for months while they move with seeming abruptness and intuition on others. They talk a great deal or are suddenly apt listeners.*

The purpose of this book has been to help managers develop that flexibility.

* Ibid.

Index